**S0-AUX-110**

FINDING YOUR COSMIC CONNECTION

Did you ever wonder why you had an affinity to a certain place, color, food, or type of person? Much of what forms our personality happens at birth—shaped by the positions of the stars and planets at that most critical moment. By understanding the aspects of the various sun signs, you can gain valuable insight into everything from your health and diet to financial matters to your most natural choice for a career or life mate. *Cosmic Connections* goes beyond the average astrology reports to provide you with a unique approach to interpreting the zodiac that is entertaining, fun—and astoundingly accurate!

COSMIC CONNECTIONS

★

Bridget Pluis

BANTAM BOOKS
NEW YORK • TORONTO • LONDON • SYDNEY • AUCKLAND

This edition contains the complete text
of the original hardcover edition.
NOT ONE WORD HAS BEEN OMITTED.

COSMIC CONNECTIONS

A Bantam Book / December 1989

PRINTING HISTORY

*Transworld Publishers edition published 1988
under the title "Bridget's Cosmic Connections"*

ISBN 0-553-28250-6

Published simultaneously in the United States and Canada

---

*Bantam Books are published by Bantam Books, a division of Bantam
Doubleday Dell Publishing Group, Inc. Its trademark, consisting of the
words "Bantam Books" and the portrayal of a rooster, is Registered in
U.S. Patent and Trademark Office and in other countries. Marca
Registrada. Bantam Books, 666 Fifth Avenue, New York, New York
10103.*

PRINTED IN THE UNITED STATES OF AMERICA

O   0   9   8   7   6   5   4   3   2   1

To Ken, Liz,
Peter, Michael, Caroline,
and Tina.

INTRODUCTION

★

Bridget's Cosmic Connections is a book that provides an insight to your Sun Sign.

Your birthday is the key to your character, and although this is only a minute part of your astrological chart, it can give accurate insights when looking at the characteristics of the Zodiac. Naturally, if you wish to have a more detailed analysis, a qualified astrologer should draw up your own individual horoscope; but for a generalized, fun interpretation, the Sun signs will provide the answers.

Each section in the book is designed to help you over the trouble spots you encounter when interacting with others, giving pointers to better living and loving.

The negative aspects of one's birth sign are too often ignored, and this chapter should help readers complement, counteract, and camouflage the less likable aspects of their Sun sign.

Young people will find the careers section helpful if they are unsure of what course to pursue in life, and they could try some of the suggestions in part-time jobs during school.

The "cusp" sign hasn't been forgotten and should

answer the questions of these signs and of those who live with or love the "cuspie." Remember, it's not easy to be two people rolled into one.

The countries of the Zodiac will open up new and exciting travel prospects, giving more understanding about why we get pulled back to favorite holiday spots.

For that yearly headache of Christmas, the section on gift giving may be the answer for that difficult-to-buy-for person.

Cosmic Connections was written in response to all the questions that come through the mailbag to my magazine column and to my talk-radio programs. It seems that most people want just enough information to be able to understand the basics of the Sun sign, without being dazzled by science. More serious students will be able to study all aspects of astrology through other learning programs.

Cosmic Connections is a lighthearted, tongue-in-cheek romp through the Sun signs and should be read in a humorous vein.

Bridget

SUN SIGN DATES

Aries
March 21 to April 20

Taurus
April 21 to May 21

Gemini
May 22 to June 21

Cancer
June 22 to July 23

Leo
July 24 to August 23

Virgo
August 24 to September 23

Libra
September 24 to October 23

Scorpio
October 24 to November 22

Sagittarius
November 23 to December 22

Capricorn
December 23 to January 20

Aquarius
January 21 to February 19

Pisces
February 20 to March 20

CONTENTS

★

BABIES OF
THE ZODIAC

ARIES

This is the first sign of the Zodiac, and Aries babies usually come into the world with a head-long rush that continues throughout life. They are loving children, but a little insecure, and often hide their true feelings behind a facade of indifference. Hats of any description appeal to them, probably because Aries rules the head; and because of their strong affinity to the Ram, they form strong attachments to their woolen blankets, trailing them everywhere they go. Toys for this sign should be action-packed: fleets of toy cars and definitely a fire engine. Miss Aries will love dolls with long hair, pretend makeup, ribbons and ponytail holders for her hair.

TAURUS

Taureans hate change and babies are no exception; loathing having to leave the snug womb, they are often late arriving. They are greedy little people and often suffer from upset tummies from guzzling too fast and too much. Venus-ruled children enjoy feeling, tasting, and touching, so Taurean babies will gain a lot of pleasure from being nursed. Parents should allow about six months before weaning, as these children balk at sudden moves. They are slow to infuriate—but stand back when they have a temper tantrum and duck the flying toy missiles! When selecting gifts for young Taureans you can't go wrong with building blocks, musical toys, books, and records.

GEMINI

Don't say I didn't warn you, when you fall into bed dog-tired after chasing this mercurial sign around all day. The trouble is, that after three hours of shut-eye, Gemini babies are raring to go again with recharged batteries, shaking the crib from its foundations and exercising their lungs to the fullest. Most parents of a Geminian child are thrilled when their offspring is the first in the street to walk and talk, but the novelty soon wears off when they're too tired to boast. Geminis' dominant theme is "I think," and they spend hours doing just this, wondering how to tie Mom and Dad up in knots. Toys that provide a mental challenge are best, such as jigsaws, Erector Sets, kites, or any educational toy.

CANCER

Moon children can be moody. They get quite emotional when left with people they don't know too well, and it's better if they can be baby-sat in their own home. Food is a security blanket to them, so parents should keep an eye on the scales. Cancer children tend to be little slobs; they gobble their food so fast, they leave half of it on the bib, and they leave a trail of discarded toys and other items as a constant reminder they've been there. Parents have a real battle on their hands when it comes to throwing out old toys, as this sign is the biggest hoarder of the Zodiac. Gifts to buy for these soft little people are buckets and shovels, bubble blowers, new swimsuits, paints, and coloring books.

LEO

Have you ever wondered, when watching your Leo cub play with the neighbors' children, why yours is the Chief and the others are the Indians? It's because this sign is a born leader and naturally puts him or herself in the lead role. Leos love an audience and will put on a star turn when the limelight's on them. Tidiness is not their forte and they'll roar with displeasure when you make them put their toys away. They are fascinated by the open flame, so put guards around the fires, shoo them away from the barbecue, and hide the matches. When they're teething they'll run high temperatures, and in summer they burn very easily. Favorite toys are any stuffed animals or new clothes.

VIRGO

Virgo babies look like little angels, but can in fact be little devils. They can be very fussy with their food and, because they are great actors and actresses, often have parents reaching for the doctor's phone number when they should be dialing the local theater school. Mercury-ruled, they love communication, and their favorite person is the family cat. Other things they enjoy are toy telephones, games, xylophones, kaleidoscopes, and nurse outfits. Not always demonstrative, they enjoy fussing over anyone that's sick. If you want to keep them amused, buy a packet of seeds and let them have their own vegetable or flower plot. As with most Earth signs, they love being outdoors.

LIBRA

Perfect strangers often stop and exclaim, ''What a beautiful baby!'' to the proud mother. Libran children usually have beautiful skin and lovely features. As this is one of the dual signs of the Zodiac, these children can often catch parents unawares with their swinging moods, and they react to unsettled conditions adversely. They show artistic traits at an early age and love to help Mom in the kitchen. Boys love toys that have movable parts: racing cars, train sets, and swings; while girls love dolls with large wardrobes, cooking sets like Mom's, and perfumed soap and talc. They'll get a great deal of enjoyment watching the family canary chatter and play. They are friendly little souls and often spend more time at the neighbors' than they do at home.

SCORPIO

Scorpio children can be an enigma to their parents when they show signs of having been here before and they act as if they're two going on two hundred. As Scorpio is the sign of reincarnation, this isn't as farfetched as it seems. When teething, these little people will often get bronchitis as well, but their recuperative powers are good. These children form strong attachments to older people, and grandparents are number one in their eyes. They are secretive and will have plenty of unseen friends to play with. They are very dramatic, so take everything they say or do with a grain of salt. They're champions of the underdog and will fight other children's battles. Toys they enjoy are model airplanes, video games, Chinese checkers, and dominoes.

SAGITTARIUS

These happy-go-lucky little souls will be the light of your life, and you'd better make the most of their kisses and cuddles while they're babies before the wanderlust catches up with them in young adulthood. Sagittarius is known as the "traveling" sign, and many a mother has lost her child in the supermarket while her back's been turned. Sagittarians have a great love affair with horses, and it's a safe bet to give them books and toys that have something to do with this animal. It's not unusual for them to pick up stray dogs and cats and bring them home. Music is food for their soul, so a radio in their room will keep them amused for hours. They hate to be confined and have a great sense of adventure.

CAPRICORN

Here is one sign you can set your clock by, especially when it's the two A.M. feed. As they become older, Capricorn's dominant theme, "I use," becomes more evident as nimble fingers take apart the most intricate toys or perform stunning hairdressing feats on dolls. Favored toys are footballs, jump ropes, Play-Doh™, trampolines, and roller skates. This is a shy and reserved sign, and Capricorns tend to worry over anything and everything. Great savers, they soon learn to keep their pocket money and use everyone else's. Privacy is important to these children, so don't worry if they appear to like their own company in preference to others. Hardworking and industrious, they love to help parents around the house or garden.

AQUARIUS

You should quit while you're ahead if you've got one of these interplanetary visitors in the house. Nonconformist children, they take great delight in getting themselves dressed, much to the consternation of Mom when she sees what they are wearing. Their taste in food is just as offbeat, and it's nothing to see the vegetables being mixed in with the fruit salad or the meat dipped in the milk. Forget the high chair at feeding time, as high places present a challenge they can't resist; and feed them while their interest is concentrated on pulling big brother's projects apart. Their inquiring minds drive parents crazy, and clocks and watches hold great fascination for them. Outdoor games or space-age toys will interest them.

PISCES

When you have psychic children like Pisceans in the house, you must learn to accept their imaginary friends at the table, out shopping, and in the bath. Dreamy little people, it's hard for parents to get them moving, and as they have a vivid imagination, they tend to embroider the truth somewhat. They are quite untidy, but are such darlings that older brothers and sisters often cover up for them. As a Water sign, anything to do with the beach delights them, and a goldfish as a present will keep them mesmerized for hours. The girls are regular little flirts and use their long-lashed eyes to the fullest advantage, while the boys are sensitive, sympathetic, and generous. Like the other Water signs, a swimming pool is a magnet, so teach them to swim at an early age.

BIRTHSTONES

Each sign is represented by its birthstone and this can be a *boon* if you're unsure what gift to buy for someone. Here is a rundown on each particular stone for the twelve months.

January

The GARNET—a beautiful deep red stone that is said to symbolize constant affection.

February

The AMETHYST—that delicate violet shade that goes with just about everything. This stone is said to enhance sincerity.

March

The BLOODSTONE—very typical of the "red" planet Mars, which rules Aries. This is said to denote courage.

April

The DIAMOND—typifying purity.

May

The EMERALD—there'd be few Taureans who wouldn't love green. Supposedly it brings hope.

June

The AGATE or PEARL—no surprise to find that this is the only month that has two stones symbolizing good health.

July

The RUBY—said to bring contentment for this birth month.

August

The SARDONYX—a not so well known stone that has reddish brown and white bands in it, said to bring fidelity.

September

The beautiful SAPPHIRE—bringing with it repentance.

October

The OPAL—is lucky for very few, this month being the exception. Actually said to symbolize good luck.

November

The TOPAZ—said to denote cheerfulness.

December

The TURQUOISE—said to bring unselfishness to the wearer.

CAREERS

★

ARIES

This Mars-ruled sign has a built-in survival kit, so usually does well in whatever he or she tackles. Ariens respond well to criticism if it's fair, discipline, and organization, and rarely flap when the pressure's on. If they are going to have a minor nervous breakdown, they'll do it in the privacy of their own home and not in front of colleagues. The public service has its share of Ariens, with nursing, teaching, and the military well served, and they make excellent enforcers of the law. Creative Ariens do well in advertising, producing radio or television shows, hairdressing, and cosmetology.

TAURUS

The building sign, as Taurus is often referred to, certainly seems to produce a lot of bricklayers, architects, builders, and real estate salespersons. Ms. Bull finds her own little niche working in banks or health insurance offices, dental nursing, or nurseries (the garden type). This is a great sign to have on the payroll, as Taureans are diligent, hardworking, loyal, and honest. It takes quite a while for them to learn something, but once it's in their head, it's there to stay. They can't be hurried and they rarely cut corners. It's this sign that brings the fresh flowers into the office to brighten it up, and Taureans love chocolate chip cookies for morning and afternoon snacks.

GEMINI

Any career that involves versatility, constant change, and mental challenges will draw Gemini to it like a magnet. Talented musicians, great school teachers, telephone operators, word processors, auctioneers, radio announcers, and salespeople, they respond well to what's required of them. This dual sign is able to handle two jobs at a time, so it's quite normal to see Geminis moonlighting at other careers. The only problem is that their enthusiasm can run out before the current job is completed, and there's often a garage full of incomplete projects. They love to play the devil's advocate, so if working alongside a Gemini, don't rise to the bait or you'll play right into their hands.

CANCER

If you're sick, then you need a Cancerian looking after you. The kind and sympathetic Crab is always ready with a box of tissues to mop up tears and a ready shoulder to lean on. No club would function without a good Cancerian cocktail waitress, and they make great flight attendants. Being real softies with animals, they do well in zoology, and their creative talents often lead them to window dressing, commercial art, cake decorating, and dress designing. As this sign is the homemaker of the Zodiac, the male will often apply himself better to the partnership than other signs if his wife is studying or working odd hours, while the female Cancerian will forgo a promising career if it conflicts with home and family.

LEO

This sign doesn't know the meaning of secondhand, second place, or second in charge. Leos set out to carve a career that has them number one. Their love of the limelight often sees them on the stage as singers or actors, while modeling and political careers draw them like a moth to a flame. If creativity isn't their bag, they enjoy being firemen, steel workers, chefs, and entrepreneurs. They work hard and play hard, so the paycheck suffers and a part-time job may be necessary. As the Sun rules their sign, they can work as lifeguards or around gardens doing odd jobs, as they are at their best in summer.

VIRGO

Every job needs a behind-the-scenes worker and Virgo is this person. With very little fuss and bother, bookwork will be done, accounts sent out on time, telephone messages dealt with, and problem clients calmed down in a quiet and efficient way. Ideally, Virgos are suited to libraries, of both records and books, being receptionists, secretaries, journalists, landscape gardeners, floral artists, and dieticians. Don't expect them to be the life of the office party; rather, get them to organize it, and if you have a few beers too many and can't remember what you said or did, get them to tell you. They are also great for getting donations from others for worthy causes.

LIBRA

If you have a Libra about to leave school and join the work force, chances are it'll be twelve months before he can make up his mind what to do. As this sign is ruled by Venus, Librans are bound to be creative, so manicurists, jewelry designers, writers, painters, and potters do well. Any career with the law, social work, or weight control also brings good results. Their charm makes them great in public relations, selling, and politics. Librans often take on a job that has odd working hours, so partners are long-suffering and get used to eating alone. They hate being cooped up in stuffy offices and are often found working outdoors or having extended lunch hours.

SCORPIO

Most Scorpios have been here before, so they can take on jobs that require skill and dedication, probably because they've already had a crack at them in another life. They make great detectives, good sports administrators, computer operators, plumbers, naval personnel, private secretaries, and dedicated doctors. The females of the species rise to great heights in their chosen careers because they know they are every bit as good as their male counterparts. They enjoy wearing a uniform, so tend to apply for jobs that require this dress. Being loners, and disliking others telling them what to do, they are better suited to being their own bosses.

SAGITTARIUS

This sign as a rule loves animals, so a Sagittarian's first choice in a career is to work with them, if possible. The A.S.P.C.A., zoos, farms, circuses, places that breed and train animals, and many a pet shop usually have a Sagittarian involved. Travel plays an important part with this person, so careers as tour guides, travel agents, or in foreign affairs and the import-export business will bring satisfying results. Like their fellow Fire sign, Leo, Sagittarians love to be seen, and the entertainment field has its share of them. Not the most tactful sign of the Zodiac, they should steer clear of jobs that require diplomacy and patience, as they tend to run on a short fuse.

CAPRICORN

Capricorn is one of the three Earth signs and usually does well in down-to-earth occupations. Butchers, gardeners, horticulturists, stonemasons, grave diggers, morticians, fencing contractors, accountants, hotel and motel managers, bakers, all earn enough money to put aside for a rainy day. Capricorns don't work well under pressure and hate to be rushed. Housebound Capricorns can earn extra pocket money by putting their creative abilities to work in knitting and sewing. It's not unusual to see a Capricorn start his or her own business later on in life when everyone else is about to retire. Capricorns usually have the first dollar they earned framed above the mantelpiece.

AQUARIUS

As soon as they are old enough to leave school, Aquarians are champing at the bit to get into the work force. Anything and everything appeals to these nonconformists, and parents often despair when their brainy offspring opt for an unconventional job. They have a head full of ideas that should be put to good use in advertising, engineering, interior decorating, sign writing, scientific work, space technology, fashion or jewelry design, electrical contracting, writing, teaching, and selling. This is the "I know" sign, so Aquarius takes to study like a duck to water, but they can be infuriating when breathing down your neck waiting for the chance to say "I knew" you shouldn't have done it that way.

PISCES

If you want to see Pisceans in their natural environment look for jobs that deal with water. Pool maintenance, selling water beds, deep-sea diving, fishing, plumbing and draining, working as refrigeration mechanics, ski instructors, laboratory technicians, oil rig workers, and professional surfers will all appeal to the men. Women prefer more creative pursuits such as acting, kindergarten teaching, or working as a masseuse, physiotherapist, cocktail waitress, or swimming instructor. Pisceans are suckers for a sad story, so spouses and parents should collect the housekeeping money from this sign before it's donated to some other worthy cause.

COUNTRIES AND
THE ZODIAC

★

People often ask me if particular countries have affinities with the Zodiac. I believe they do, and it is accepted that the following signs and countries bear some resemblance.

ARIES

Aries is said to tie in with England, Germany, Denmark, and Israel. Each one of these countries has had its share of battles fought in and around it, and the Danes were a force to be reckoned with. This isn't surprising, as Aries is ruled by Mars, the "fighting planet." Its quality is masculine and positive; its planetary principle is action, and its primal desire is leadership. No wonder these countries come under close scrutiny by others that are preparing to invade. The English reserve, German stolidity, the cold Danish, and fiery Israeli nature all reflect the moods of Aries. Any monetary gain is efficiently rechanneled back into arms and defense by the countries' leaders and, like their Aries counterparts, these countries are very rarely seen without their protective armor. Very few scandals are heard of from these countries, and any that may come to the surface, like the Christine Keeler affair, are quickly and efficiently dealt with.

TAURUS

Ireland, Poland, Iran, and some parts of the Soviet Union are said to be associated with Taurus. The Bull is a hardworking animal very close to nature, and the countries it represents seem to consist of hardworking people, many of them spending their days in the fields. Taurus hates change and rebels violently against it. (Hence the fighting in Iran and war-torn Ireland.) Like any Taurean, these countries will take a lot to start them fighting, but once riled, watch out. It's a devastating sight to see an angry Bull in full flight. They are all countries that keep themselves to themselves, like the Taurus person who has plenty of acquaintances but very few close friends. Those that are given friendship must comply with the rules that Taurus sets down.

GEMINI

The United States of America, Belgium, and Wales are said to belong to the sign of Gemini. Very applicable when you think of America being split in two with the Civil War and racial problems from the first day white man set foot on Indian land, to this day with the blacks. Where else would you hear the tongue being given such a workout as in the United States? Watergate was a good example. Wales is a country where, unless you are Welsh, you've got no hope of keeping up with the language. The material factor of Gemini is invention, and certainly the United States can be given full marks for this. Gemini's theme is "I think," and one of America's most loved presidents, John F. Kennedy, was born under the sign of Gemini. Communication is the keyword, and as the space probes delve deeper and deeper into outer space, we open up our channels of communication. Already, thanks to the United States, we can now link up to that country through satellite.

CANCER

New Zealand, Scotland, Holland, and Paraguay are the countries that belong to Cancer. Love and security are the planetary principle and primal desire of Cancer, and it's interesting to note how many natives of these countries retrace their footsteps and settle down with their families after the wanderlust has left them. Most of these countries are known for their beautiful lakes, hot springs, or dykes showing the affinity of the Water sign Cancer. The countries mentioned keep out of the limelight as much as possible and even tend to live in the past. They are not interested in keeping up with fashion, content to meander slowly through life, taking each day as it comes.

LEO

The most prominently identifiable countries with Leo are said to be France, Italy, and Rumania. Each country personifies the color, excitement, and love of living life to the fullest that Leos have. The planetary principle of Leo is creativity, and every one of these countries has produced more than one brilliant sculptor, musician, or dancer. The quality of Leo is fixed and masculine, and again one can look at the dominant role the male plays in each country. Leos are ruled by the heart, and France especially is linked with affairs of the heart. The volatile temper can be attributed to Leo and Mt. Vesuvius; and the general feeling that the French, Italians, and Rumanians have about the importance of their families is reflected in every Leo.

VIRGO

Of all the countries said to be identified with Virgo, Switzerland is probably the closest. Many New England states in the United States are said to be Virgoan, particularly Virginia, and undoubtedly,

Boston. All these places are refined, cool, calm, and unflappable. Like most Virgos, these places don't like attention being drawn to them and, if asked to give an opinion, prefer to stay neutral. The planetary principle is purity, the quality is negative and feminine. The material factor is service and this is given unstintingly and thoroughly. Swiss watches are renowned for their efficiency, and Boston is renowned for its respectability. Scandal is mostly unheard of, and a visit to any of these places would be like most Virgos: bland, pleasant, extremely easy on the eye, but dull.

LIBRA

Austria, China, Argentina, and a great portion of the Far East can be attributed to Libra. Diplomacy is one of the keywords that Libra understands and certainly has to be used in one or more of the countries mentioned. The sense of balance so important to Libra can be seen in China's attitude to each person getting an equal share of wealth, or so it is thought. The primal desire of Libra is union, and China would probably be more in favor of this than a lot of the other Libra-ruled countries. The love of meditation and higher philosophies is clearly shown in Tibet and Burma, while Argentina provides the music and dancing very close to the Libran heart.

SCORPIO

Norway, Algeria, and Morocco all come under the Scorpio grouping. Little can be said about these countries in comparison to Scorpio unless one makes the point that it's either fire or ice when dealing with a Scorpio. The Scorpion, being completely at home in the desert, probably leads its share of Scorpios to follow careers in the hot desert countries. Mystery has always shrouded Morocco and is reflected in the dark brooding glances of the Scorpio person. The planetary principle of Scorpio is power, the primal desire is to control, and the material factor is to rise above.

SAGITTARIUS

Spain, Saudi Arabia, Hungary, and Australia are all supposed to be attuned to Sagittarius. The bullring is a natural place for Sagittarians to meet. The color red and the excitement of the Bull—a sign which Sagittarians have little affinity with—is exactly what fires this sign's soul. Australia, with its outdoor involvement and its easygoing attitudes, reflects the Sagittarian temperament. The love of horses again comes through another of the countries Sagittarius is attributed to, Arabia. The Arab bloodstock business is doing very well in Australia. The primal desire of Sagittarius is liberty, the planetary principle is expansion, and the material factor is growth. What better place than Australia for Sagittarians to feel at home?

CAPRICORN

India, Albania, Bulgaria, and Greece are the countries most prominently associated with Capricorn. The moral code of this sign is reflected in all of these countries, where reserve and decorum are taught from an early age. Like most Capricorns, these countries are full of hardworking, down-to-earth people, who wear the somber colors favored by this sign for work, but for special occasions they bring out the bright plumage. The primal desire of Capricorn is attainment and the material factor is materialization. Like their sign, these countries know that only hard work will bring rewards to them. Capricorns are said to be the most successful in gardening and cultivation, particularly of starchy foods like potatoes and rice, and the above countries would use a fair amount of this with the exception, perhaps, of Greece.

AQUARIUS

The U.S.S.R. and Sweden are identified with Aquarius. Like the sign, they have to be handled delicately for fear of setting off a fuse. The Aquarian's love of science and adventure can be seen readily both in the U.S.S.R., with the space program, and in Sweden, with its fearless seafarers. Nonconformist in love, Sweden often reflects the Aquarius way of thinking. The planetary principle is truth, the primal desire is to know and understand, and the material factor is investigation. Little wonder that Russia's K.G.B. strikes fear into the heart of any would-be spy. The Aquarius love of humanity is recognized in the ideals expressed by the U.S.S.R. We may not agree with their policies, but we must agree that they look after their old. A very Aquarian trait.

PISCES

Portugal, Scandinavia, and, to a lesser degree, the small Mediterranean islands are said to belong to Pisces. It seems fitting that these countries have rarely had any adverse publicity. Content to let the rest of the world fight, like Pisces, these places are happy in the background. With beautiful scenery and a gentle disposition, the people of these countries regard love as an important part of life. The planetary principle of Pisces is sacrifice, the primal desire is unification, and the material factor is love. Anyone who knows a Pisces will see every one of these attributes in their makeup. The quieter life, the enjoyment of the simple pleasures of life, and the "what will be, will be" attitude that can be found in these countries with their warm and loving inhabitants reflect the relaxed nature of Pisces. The fact that there is plenty of water and ice around shows the affinity to the Water sign.

CUSP SIGNS

UNDERSTANDING THE CUSP SIGNS

First of all, what is a "cusp" sign? It's the dividing line between two houses or signs, usually agreed upon as beginning a few days before the end of the outgoing sign and ending a few days after the beginning of the incoming sign.

People born within this time are often at a loss as to what sign they really are. I personally feel that one throws back to the departing sign's characteristics much more, even if born actually two or three days into the new sign. Those born on the cusp often wonder why they are at conflict with themselves; but they are two different people rolled into one and therefore should read the characteristics of both signs to fully understand themselves.

29

That's not bad, you know. At least if you don't like what the daily star forecasts give you for one side of your nature, you can have a second chance for your other side. Most people born on the cusp manage to live fairly peaceably with their other nature, but every now and again the dominant side of their cusp takes over and can turn a normally quiet person into a force to be reckoned with. This is seen quite often with the Cancer/Leo cusp and the Pisces/Aries cusp. When looking for a soul mate, the cusp sign often strikes more trouble than the "true" sign. The best bet here is to find another cusp sign. This balances out the two sides of both natures.

ARIES/TAURUS
April 18–23

To understand this cusp sign, you must look at the two signs individually, then blend them together.

Okay, so we know we can pull the wool over an Aries' eyes and Taurus is a lot of Bull, but what else? Let's look at the negative side of this combination. Noise, and plenty of it, is one of the hurdles to get over. The bleating, bellowing, and stamping of hooves when this combination throws a tantrum can daunt the most courageous adversary, but it's mostly noise.

People with this cusp tend to lower their horns and rush in, because the Taurus side is shortsighted, and consequently they end up with egg on their faces. Cowardice is another slight problem. Don't get me wrong; in the face of disaster, Ariens are champions and heroes, but take them to the dentist and they definitely need the stoical Taurus to hold their hands. The Aries nature tends to have a few hangups, usually due to insecurity and because members of this sign are born worriers.

On the bright side, this duo has a lot going for it. Born organizers, the pair of them; blend them and you've got a regular five-star general. Don't visit this cusp sign and expect to lie in bed until midday. Not on your life! It's a household run with military precision, the wash marching across the line at seven A.M. and all socks, undies, and dishtowels together. No dust is ever seen in this household. Mr. Aries/Taurus loves to be boss, especially if he's in the type of job where a uniform is required. He waves his arms around a lot and gives plenty of orders, but no one really takes him seriously. Ms. Ram-ble is very overprotective due to her Aries cusp nature, but she covers this well with the Taurus "no-nonsense" attitude.

Sexually a great twosome. The fire and drama of Aries, added to the sensuality and basic earthiness of Taurus, and you've got one hell of a lover. A few words of warning, however: lead, don't push, this cusp sign. Point out what you'd like to do tactfully, but whatever you do, don't give ultimatums. Being downright ornery critters, people with this cusp will dig their little hooves into terra firma and refuse to budge.

Compatible signs for an Aries/Taurus cusp sign would be Libra/Scorpio cusp, Sagittarius/Capricorn cusp, and Leo/Virgo cusp.

Famous personalities born on this cusp are Jayne Mansfield, Queen Elizabeth II, Adolf Hitler, William Shakespeare, Shirley Temple Black, Charlotte Brontë, Anthony Quinn, Napoleon III.

TAURUS/GEMINI
May 19–24

Anyone who is born within this cusp area knows they are dealing with three and not two characteristics. This is because Gemini is a "dual" sign and when blended with Taurus gives a three-dimensional aspect.

The practical, mulish nature of Taurus more often than not throws its hands in the air with disgust when the irrepressible Gemini side cuts loose. What can any self-respecting Taurean do when faced with the zany sense of humor and love of practical jokes that makes up a Gemini?

One could liken it to a parent/child relationship, the Taurean being the steadying influence over the Geminian unknown quantity. It's the Gemini side that gets this cusp sign into trouble and it's usually up to Taurus to rectify it. This sign is no fool when it comes down to the nitty gritty and the two key phrases—Taurus "I have" and Gemini

"I think"—make for a very good long-term planner. Taurus is the builder of the Zodiac and never makes a move unless the foundations are solid and security is guaranteed. However, Taureans do strike trouble when the Gemini cusp rebels and throws ready-made Taurus plans into confusion. Quite often this cusp combination moves home and job frequently, not to mention romance. When this cusp sign shows signs of erupting, head for the hills. The Taurean temper is a sight to behold; couple this with the Gemini verbosity, and it's high time you were nowhere to be seen.

Moods can also be a problem with this cusp sign, so if they don't want to be sociable, don't nag. They'll make up for it later, so make the most of the peace and quiet. Males try very hard to be macho, but because they are children at heart, thanks to the Gemini influence they never really put on a believable performance.

Sexually, you never know what to expect. Geminis hate routine and believe the adage "variety is the spice of life," so their love life is far from dull. A born flirt, this cusp courts disaster without even meaning to. Luckily, both signs have the gift of the gab and this gets the cusp out of hot water.

Compatible signs for this cusp would be Scorpio/ Sagittarius, Pisces/Aries, Virgo/Libra.

Famous personalities born on this cusp are Queen Victoria, Laurence Olivier, Marshal Tito, James Stewart, Margot Fonteyn.

GEMINI/CANCER
June 19–24

Have you heard the old saying "as deep as the ocean and as high as the sky"? Well, that's what you've got if you're born on the cusp of Gemini/Cancer. If you think you can't understand yourself, spare a thought for those poor people around you; they have no hope.

Let's see if we can pin this elusive sign down long enough to analyze it. Gemini has a mind like quicksilver and expends all its energy running around getting nowhere fast, usually leaving a trail of destruction. Cancer surveys the scene, shrugs the shoulders, and heads for the fridge. Food and drink play an important role in the Cancer cusp. As a result, it's usually the Gemini side that decides to jog to keep the fat at bay. This person is devilish and loves to tease, but there's no malice intended. People belonging to this cusp have lots of friends and make very good parents. Home and family play an important part, and as long as there's a pool in the backyard, they are happy to entertain at home.

The male cusp sign sings loudly in the shower, gives lots of orders, fusses about nothing, and has strange eating habits. The female cusp cries at sad movies, is clever with her hands, and like her male counterpart, likes to get up on a soapbox to put a point of view across. Combine all these attributes and you'll get a very wet bag of wind who promises the earth and delivers compost. Members of this sign often have champagne tastes on a beer salary, but they mean well.

Sexually a restless sign, not necessarily unfaithful, but it does need room to move. The Gemini loves constant stimulation while Cancer looks for an emotional involvement. Whatever you do, don't have a fight with this cusp sign before going to bed. Gemini will give you back as good as they get, and Cancer will throw a bucket of cold water on your ardor.

Compatible signs for this cusp would be Scorpio/Sagittarius, Capricorn/Aquarius, and Aries/Taurus. Famous personalities born on this cusp are the Duchess of Windsor, Errol Flynn, Jane Russell, Michele Lee, Jack Dempsey, and Lionel Ritchie.

CANCER/LEO
July 21–26

This is not an easy combination to live with by any stretch of the imagination. How would you like to think like a lion and have the Cancer side of you scuttle sideways like the crab every time you decide to act?

This is a Water/Fire cusp sign, so most red hot ideas end up as damp squibs.

When the Lion roars everyone takes notice, but this is nothing compared to the nip that the Crab can inflict when cornered. This cusp sign has a heart as big as a bucket and makes a great friend.

Loyalty and sympathy are two of this sign's strongest points, but negative traits are vanity, gullibility, and extravagance. Pride is often the downfall for members of this cusp, as they hate to be proved wrong, so much so that they tend to go overboard and then have to go and lick their wounds in private.

As with the other strong/weak signs, the Leo side of this sign's nature probably overrules the quieter Cancerian side. This can be unfortunate in a job because the bossy Leo nature may grate on workmates and get their backs up. The male tends to be a peacock, flashy, arrogant, and domineering; he often gets himself into situations that the Cancer side of his nature doesn't know how to handle. The female is an excellent mother, loving, sympathetic, and hardworking. Every now and again the Lioness comes out and she bares her teeth and sharpens her claws, but only when her loved ones are threatened.

Very attractive, this cusp sign has no trouble attracting the opposite sex. The flame of Leo draws them close and the claws of the Crab hold them. Sexually this sign seeks a strong yet tender partner and in return will give undying love, devotion, and respect. Never poke fun at this cusp sign's performance or you'll have a sulky, snarly wildcat on your hands.

Compatible signs for this cusp sign would be Pisces/Aries, Sagittarius/Capricorn, Taurus/Gemini. Famous personalities that share this cusp date are

Sir Edmund Hillary, Isaac Stern, Natalie Wood, Amelia Earhart, Ernest Hemingway, George Bernard Shaw.

LEO/VIRGO
August 21–26

If you had to choose a nurse or doctor, you couldn't go past members of this cusp sign. They are sympathetic, gentle, and long-suffering; in fact, one of our nicer cusp combinations.

The drive and ambition of Leo is tempered by the cool, analytical approach of Virgo and this level-headed outlook sees them climbing the ladder of success at a rapid rate. Negative points would be the acid tongue that is a trademark of Virgo, plus the arrogance and bossiness that comes from the Leo side. You wouldn't dare countermand this cusp's orders or you'd get out with, at the very least, a flea in your ear. Get this person mad and you have the combination of a volcano erupting and a hurricane blowing. Virgo loves to sit on the sidelines while Leo loves the limelight, so this cusp sign never really knows how she or he will react at a given time.

The male cusp sign flirts like mad, has a zany sense of humor, and enjoys the best food and wine money can buy. He usually drives an expensive but not flashy car. *She* is meticulous about her grooming, visits her hairdresser at least once a week, and has the cleanest children in the street.

Ask this cusp sign for honest advice only if you can stand the cold hard facts because it will pull no punches and give it to you straight.

Sexually, those with this cusp expect back what they give. There are no half measures, only faithfulness and an open frank attitude with no sordid extramarital encounters. Unfortunately, the Leo side of their natures causes them to wear their hearts on their sleeves and at times this rebounds on them.

Compatible partners for this sign would be Aquarius/Pisces, Libra/Scorpio and Taurus/Gemini. Famous names who share this cusp date are Emily Brontë, Princess Margaret, Gene Kelly, Van Johnson, Mel Ferrer, Leonard Bernstein, Claude Debussy, and Count Basie.

VIRGO/LIBRA
September 21–26

This is probably the best way to be a Libra. At least with the steadying influence of a Virgo Earth sign hanging round constantly, there's more chance of keeping this sign's feet on the ground. The flights of fancy are more practical, and when it comes to putting them into practice, the methodical Virgo side makes sure it's followed through.

Negative points, without a doubt, would be the weighing and balancing Libra does constantly and the analyzing that Virgo does. Don't expect these people to give a snap decision; they have to process all the ifs, buts, and maybes before they make a move.

Let's stop a moment and look at this sign's temper. It's no good saying it doesn't have one. Libra is finely balanced at the best of times, but throw on a clod of earth and you're in big trouble. Out come the black scowls, the Mercury-ruled quicksilver mood changes that Virgos are known for; add this to the swirling air currents that Libra puts out, and you've got the makings of a beaut of a storm. Members of this cusp get a bit upset if you point out their failings, too. The great things about this sign are the obvious talents with music, theatre, and art.

Mr. Virgo/Libra can be a bit of a pain at times; he expects a lot from his partner and picks everything to bits when he gets home. On the social scale he'd rate ten out of ten, but at home he'd be no help at all. Ms. Virgo/Libra is a little more reliable. She rarely goes out for coffee mornings or visits neighbors. Study is important to her, so quite often she'll busy herself with a hobby or take a course.

Sexually, those with this cusp may be at sixes and sevens with their feelings. Cool, calm Virgo tries to analyze the changing emotions that flit through the Libran mind. Like most Air signs, Libra will seek constant change to offset boredom—just the opposite of the down-to-earth Virgo.

Compatible signs would be the following cusp

signs: Capricorn/Aquarius, Scorpio/Sagittarius, Gemini/Cancer.

Famous names born around the same cusp date are Barbara Walters, Mickey Rooney, Olivia Newton-John, Larry Hagman, Anne of Cleves, George Gershwin, David McCallum.

LIBRA/SCORPIO
October 21–26

Oh, boy, now we've got trouble! High-flying Libra combined with moody, dramatic Scorpio.

Passions run high with this cusp combination. Hot or cold, black or white, there's no middle line. All or nothing; so if you know one of these people, you'll either have a very good friend or a bitter enemy. Great fighters for lost causes, they take on the whole world's problems when, needless to say, they have plenty of their own. Negative points in this combination would be jealousy and possessiveness from the Scorpio side doing constant battle with the Libran logic and flirtatious nature.

Can you imagine what must go on in these minds when they go to a party? Scorpio looks around the room and says "Mmm, I like the look of him/her. I might try to get them away from their partner just for the hell of it." Libra comes in as the conscience, putting a damper on the idea, moralizing, chiding, and usually winning.

Positive points would have to be empathy, tenderness, and fair play. Good looks abound with this cusp sign and its members seem to have more than everyone else.

Mr. Libra/Scorpio is a distinct worry, moving with pantherlike speed, a tongue dripping with honey, and a line that gets the opposite sex in, hook, line, and sinker. He's like a spider waiting for a fly, and once caught, his prey will have no hope of escape. Ms. Libra/Scorpio is only a little less overpowering. Her sultry looks, lively patter, bubbling personality and typical Scorpio magnetism attract the males, and no other girl in the room has a chance. Once she's caught them she loses interest, and many a poor man has been unceremoniously dumped and never known why.

Sexually a torrid combination. Not for them the mundane, once-a-week routine. Spice, passion, and excitement are on the agenda here. Never try to work out what makes this person tick. Just sit back and enjoy it.

Compatible signs are Aquarius/Pisces, Taurus/Gemini, Cancer/Leo. Well-known names that share this cusp date are Franz Liszt, Sarah Bernhardt, Catherine Deneuve, Johann Strauss, Pablo Picasso, Theodore Roosevelt, Johnny Carson.

SCORPIO/SAGITTARIUS
November 20–25

One thing's for sure: what you see is what you get with this cusp sign. No frills, no nonsense, and nearly no friends. This is because they haven't heard the old sayings, "discretion is the better part of valor" or "look before you leap." All they've heard is "a bird in the hand etc." or "it's now or never."

Mothers-in-law who are born on this cusp combination are always in strife, the Scorpio side making them overpossessive and organizing, and the Sagittarius side speaking first and thinking later.

Positive points would be a friendly nature, a love of animals, and a clever business head. If animals leave you cold, forget about making time with anyone of this sign. It's love me, love my dog, cat, horse, bird, etc. People with this cusp love to take a gamble, whether financially or with life, so anyone who worries about the budget won't last long. They are givers much more than receivers, and they are often in trouble with their partners because of this.

Mr. Scorpio/Sagittarius has his own philosophy: the more the merrier. Consequently, he's always in trouble. He looks on life as a smorgasbord and takes whatever is in reach. He's not a certain starter in the marriage stakes—could be classed as a sprinter—as he doesn't show much staying potential. Ms. Scorpio/Sagittarius is a mixed bag, endlessly seeking the greener grass on the other side of the fence. However, once she's tied down, she applies herself to her lot with good-natured tenacity.

Sexually, you won't go far wrong with this combination. Scorpio brings in the passion, and it doesn't take too many sparks from the Sagittarius fire to ignite this one. What's more, this sign understands others' needs for freedom. Compatible cusp signs would be Pisces/Aries, Virgo/Libra, Gemini/Cancer.

Interesting people born on this cusp date include Natalia Makarova, Indira Gandhi, Robert F. Kennedy, Charles de Gaulle, Boris Karloff, Harpo Marx, Toulouse-Lautrec.

SAGITTARIUS/CAPRICORN
December 20–25

This is a typical "would be if could be, but mostly don't" sign.

Sagittarius gives the green light, but Capricorn puts on the brakes. Caution is a keyword with Capricorn, so this cusp is plagued by conservative approaches. You can imagine how Sagittarius feels about this. Just when the party's taking off and it's time to let the hair down, in comes Capricorn, the voice of gloom and doom.

The self-made businessman often comes under this cusp sign. The extroverted Sagittarius side runs ahead distributing sweetness and light, conning everyone into parting with their hard-earned cash, and Capricorn brings up the rear complete with bank statement and checkbook. This person shows great perception, often surprising family and friends with his or her ability to see beneath the surface.

Mr. Cusp is witty, but his humor often has a sardonic twist to it. He has a roving eye, but his Capricorn side makes him toe the line, so his flirting usually boils down to all talk and no action. Spotlessly clean, he can be a real bore picking up after less tidy partners. He is ambitious and rises quite rapidly to respected positions. Being part horse and part goat, he often ends up with a small country property where he can be put out to pasture when he retires. The female has a constant battle with her two sides, one keeping the weight at bay and the other curbing the expensive tastes and flamboyant colors Sagittarius loves. Sexually this sign is two completely different people. One night happy and loving with no hangups, the next night prudish, fussy, and uninterested. It's a bit like a lottery, you never know when your number is going to come up lucky. Never ridicule this sign's performance, as its ego is quickly deflated and it will take it as a personal affront.

Ideal soul mates for this cusp sign would be Gemini/Cancer, Leo/Virgo, Aries/Taurus.

Famous people who share the same date are Chris Evert, Jane Fonda, Joseph Stalin, Ava Gardner, Benjamin Disraeli, Humphrey Bogart, Barbara Mandrell, Sir Isaac Newton.

CAPRICORN/AQUARIUS
January 18–23

You can expect a few problems with this cusp combination. Here we have quiet introspective Capricorn just trying to get on with the job at hand, not making waves, in fact hoping no one will notice, and what happens! Along comes Aquarius with nonconformist, zany, unpredictable moods, and from there on, you can expect the unexpected. This is the little devil who speaks when it's not supposed to, and generally manages to make a disturbance.

In the middle of exams, while the hardworking Capricorn has the head down and tail up, the Aquarius side gets bored and the concentration is gone. The tough part about being born on this cusp is the fact that money has a habit of trickling through the fingers, thanks to the Aquarius side, and the tendency to see humor in situations where no one else does. It's nothing for this sign to be sitting in a crowded place and let out a giggle when something tickles its fancy. It nearly always happens when it's deathly quiet or in church.

Clothes present a problem too. The conservative styles and colors Capricorn prefers are the complete opposite of what an Aquarian likes to wear. Consequently, it can be a headache getting dressed for a party.

The male cusp can be found at car rallies, pubs, clubs, in fact, anywhere a deal can be drummed up. Not a moment is wasted without a business deal being sounded out. This fellow is a woman's nightmare. On the surface he appears to be practical, reliable, and faithful, but when you deal with the other side of his cusp, the Aquarian nature, you may find his wings haven't been clipped and he may not come home to roost. The female is a sweetie. A born worrier, she will invent a problem if there isn't one. She's a great mother, spending a lot of time with her children, yet keeping her finger on the pulse of the home. She's quite apt to get up at midnight and repaper the bathroom or do something equally crazy, but that's the Aquarian nature.

Compatible signs for this cusp would be Scorpio/Sagittarius, Aries/Taurus, Virgo/Libra. Famous people who share this cusp date are Cary Grant, Danny Kaye, General Robert E. Lee, Edgar Allan Poe, Telly Savalas, Jack Nicklaus, Yehudi Menuhin, Dolly Parton.

AQUARIUS/PISCES
February 17–22

There's nothing nicer than enjoying the water, but when a squall blows up suddenly, the going gets very rough. This is a very similar scenario to dealing with the Aquarius/Pisces cusp sign.

Most of the time this person remains on an even keel, and the Pisces side sends up heartfelt thanks. Aquarius, on the other hand, loves to stir, creating disturbances just to keep the dreamy Water sign on its toes. The grandiose plans of Aquarius often turn into large scale productions once the fertile imagination of Pisces gets hold of them.

Negative points would be the inability to take criticism, the ever-present insecurity, and a total disregard for finance. What they don't know won't hurt them, members of this sign reason, so don't spoil their day by waving the overdraft at them as they come through the front door.

On the brighter side, we have a sentimental, sympathetic softie who is a sucker for a sad story. This is the sign that gives away its last dollar, forgetting charity begins at home. People with this cusp are probably the most frustrating of all the cusp signs; one minute you could throttle them, and then they do something really sweet and take the wind out of your sails.

Mr. Cusp loves to be needed and likes nothing better than to wait on others. He's mother's darling, a child's soul mate, and a girl's headache. He's totally unaware of time, forgetful, and extravagant; and yet once he's got you, you can't get him out from under your skin. Ms. Cusp talks a lot, ties up the telephone for hours, is a champion at body language, and embroiders the truth in a charming way. She knows exactly who she wants and where she's heading.

Sexually a romantic at heart, this sign is easily hurt. It takes them a long time to trust again, and they will often play the field, giving a wrong impression.

Compatible signs would be Gemini/Cancer, Libra/Scorpio, Pisces/Aries.

You share your cusp date with these well-known people: Alan Bates, Jack Palance, Merle Oberon, Sidney Poitier, George Washington, Frederic Chopin, Edna St. Vincent Millay, John Mills.

PISCES/ARIES
March 18–23

What puts out a fire quicker than anything? Water, of course. There's nothing more annoying for this sign than to be fired up and then to hear an insistent little voice put a damper on things. Luckily for the Aries side, this sign doesn't take too kindly to its plans being thwarted, but goes ahead anyway, and Pisces has to be content with making a lot of steam.

This is no time to get clever if you have one of these cusp signs in tow; beneath that calm exterior lies a red-blooded fighter. The Aries side is just what's needed to get the lazy, dreamy Pisces motivated. If it weren't for the close proximity of the Aries side, this sign would drift aimlessly without direction, which would be a shame, as its members are really very talented.

If you catch this person on one of their "off" days, you'll wonder what hit you. The aloof, moralistic Aries combined with moody Pisces will make you feel as though you are dealing with an alien from another planet. If this sign goes to bat for you, you'll score a home run. You wouldn't find a more tireless worker for lost causes and the patience this sign has with the very young, infirm, or incapacitated has to be seen to be believed. Unfortunately, members of this sign are often let down, due to the trusting nature of Pisces.

Mr. Pisces/Aries is usually very busy trying to make a good impression. He longs to be liked and accepted and will go to great lengths to attain this. He doesn't suffer fools gladly and frowns upon those exploiting others. Ms. Cusp is easily hurt, acid-tongued at times, and very shy. She is great at school fairs or helping out with charity affairs.

Sexually, a marvelous cusp combination, with the fire and passion of Aries and the softness and sensitivity of Pisces. Don't make the mistake of revealing past conquests though, or you'll never hear the end of it.

Compatible signs are Capricorn/Aquarius, Sagittarius/Capricorn, Aquarius/Pisces.

Well-known Pisces/Aries cusp people include Rimsky-Korsakov, Patrick McGoohan, Sir Michael Redgrave, Doris Day, Joan Crawford.

FASHION BY
THE STARS

★

Fashion can be very fickle, not always catering to the particular likes and dislikes characteristic to our signs. However, if we know how to make the best of our good points, it is a lot easier to keep in step with fashion trends.

ARIES

The sign of the Ram usually feels very much at home in wool or wool blend materials. Well-cut skirts, slacks, and trousers are a must in any Aries wardrobe, and teamed with pure wool cardigans and sweaters, they help cut a very elegant figure. Understated elegance is often the theme and loud colors or bold patterns send Ariens in the opposite direction.

51

As is the case with many Ariens, their particular job may have them working in a uniform or perhaps with others around them who have to wear it, as in nursing, teaching, or any of the armed forces. Consequently, their leisure wear must be comfortable, light, and bright. Very rarely do they opt for the yellows and reds of their co-Fire signs, but if they do, it's usually in accessories rather than the whole outfit. Most Ariens are very fussy about their headgear, and hats and hairdos are an important and very necessary part of their wardrobe. Fashion no-nos are cheap jewelry and perfume, plunging necklines, and scuffed shoes. Well-known Ariens are Gloria Steinem, Thomas Jefferson, Loretta Lynn, Jessica Lange, and Pearl Bailey.

TAURUS

Like my fellow Taureans, I often look enviously at people who can wear trendy fashions, or ultrafeminine designs, but because many born under this sign are big-boned and can become overweight at the mere thought of pastry, unfortunately we have to stick to the more conventional lines. Luckily for Taureans, they have an unerring eye for good taste, and they wear tailored lines to perfection. Being Venus-ruled, touch and smell come high on the list of priorities when they go shopping for a new outfit. Suede, velvet, and silk will take up three quarters of a Taurean wardrobe, while they wouldn't feel fully dressed without a subtle perfume or after-shave to complete their outfit.

Colors often lean to the earth tones such as russet, varying shades of brown, green, beige, and blue. Red is usually relegated to the bedroom, especially if it's satin. Young Taureans often make the mistake of buying layered outfits, hoping to conceal their bulk, but this is the wrong way to go about it. A-line dresses will flatter, and long boxy blazers and jackets will camouflage those generous hips. Well-known Taureans are Barbra Streisand, Shirley Temple Black, Queen Elizabeth II, and Anthony Quinn.

GEMINI

One very rarely finds fat Geminis, probably because they are forever on the go, and this makes them envied by those who cannot get away with the latest fashions. Their dominant theme is "I think," and this enables them to mix and match their outfits, cleverly coming up with many variations on an old theme. White is an invaluable asset for a Gemini's wardrobe and this, teamed with blue, lemon, or black, gives extra mileage. Geminis adore jewelry and don't feel fashion is complete without it. Because many Geminis have the type of job that involves travel, wash-and-wear outfits are a must. It is typical of their duality that Geminis often lead two separate lives, and this can be seen in the complete contrast of their day and night clothes. Parties are strictly for having fun, and the gear they wear is usually zany, colorful, and a conversation piece. Well-known Geminis are Brooke Shields, Judy Garland, Marilyn Monroe, and Paul McCartney.

CANCER

Your usual Cancerians are all for putting comfort before fashion. Ask them what their favorite outfit is, and they'll reply without hesitating that it is faded old jeans, worn-out slippers, and a moth-eaten sweater or cardigan. Trying to prize those little claws off these disreputable articles is a waste of time, as most Cancerians feel at home with the past, and sentimentality is alive and well in both male and female alike.

Cancerians are ruled by the Moon, and quite often their figures bear this out. This can pose problems with outfits that have belts, making them look a little like a sack tied in the middle. Males often have a paunch. Brief bikinis, pleated skirts, and tight shorts should be avoided. Most Cancerians have beautiful eyes that often reflect the color of the garment being worn, so this feature should be highlighted. They also love fashions that have an old-fashioned theme, particularly if reminiscent of the Victorian era. It's quite probable they've hung on to them for that long, too. Well-known Cancerians include Mariette Hartley, Red Skelton, and Diana, Princess of Wales.

LEO

Bold, bossy Leos love to be seen and heard, and their taste in fashion often reflects this. Not for them the dull or cheap outfits, and they'd rather go without than be seen in something second-rate or secondhand. Many Lionesses are good seamstresses; this way they can save money and at the same time look original. Clothes that show off the body beautiful are a must, so the cut must accentuate the good features and play down the bad ones.

Colors must be warm and vibrant, to reflect the personality, particularly in winter, as Leos dislike the cold. Gold is their preference in jewelry, unless of course they are flaming redheads, in which case they may opt for silver. Trendy fashion labels are usually prominently displayed and designer purses are necessary accessories. They wear their clothes very well, as most Leos have a very erect carriage and good posture. They have to learn to live within their means at an early age or they'll overspend on clothes and get into debt. If they can marry a millionaire, all the better. Famous people born under the sign of Leo are Coco Chanel, Jackie Onassis, Lucille Ball, and Peter O'Toole.

VIRGO

This sign is often better off designing fashions than wearing them. Virgos' cool, analytical approach and ability to criticize enables them to see flaws where others can't. Practicality is the key-note on which Virgos build their wardrobes, pre-ferring to pay a little more for goods that will give them value for money. Most Virgo women will have a "basic black" dress that will see them through any function. Very rarely do you see them going for accessories like flowers in the hair, disco purses, or chunky jewelry. If you must give a Virgo a bag or wallet, make sure it's real leather not imitation.

Favorite colors are silver, blue, brown, or gray. Their styles tend to be a little severe at times, and Virgos must take care not to fall into the dull category. A word of warning: don't take a Virgo shopping with you and then ask for advice about the article you try on. You'll get it straight be-tween the eyes. Famous Virgos include Sophia Loren, Ingrid Bergman, Lily Tomlin, and Lauren Bacall.

LIBRA

Libra subjects are usually endowed with very good looks and a good body to go with it. Their love of balance is reflected in the outfits they wear and the colors are always harmonious. They prefer to be underdressed than overdressed, relying on their physical attributes to get them by. The men nearly always look good as their long legs and spare frame make it easy for them to buy ready-to-wear clothes.

Ms. Libra often has a cleavage that other women are jealous of, and she accentuates this by wearing plunging necklines or flattering colors. Librans should take care not to fall into the trap of looking flashy when striving to look attractive, as the line between these two is very thin. If a Libra invites you on a shopping spree, allow all day. Librans just can't make up their minds and this is often the way their fashions look. Favorite colors are coral, black, blue, and beige. Well-known Librans include Brigitte Bardot, Julie Andrews, Susan Sarandon, and Charlton Heston.

SCORPIO

This sign likes to attack when no one's looking, so fashions that have a delayed reaction on the opposite sex are very popular. For instance, Ms. Scorpio will have at least one skirt in her wardrobe that shows glimpses of her leg that leave a man wondering if he did or *didn't* see her leg. Men go for macho after-shave and shirts that expose the manly chest. Scorpios should wear striking colors such as burgundy, plum, navy blue, and red. At some stage in Scorpios' lives they will have had a favorite red article, but as they grow older, they tend to take red in lesser doses.

Ms. Scorpio will spend a great deal on lingerie, whereas the male Scorpio likes nothing better than to go *au naturel* to bed. The motto of Scorpios when it comes to fashion is "tease and tempt," but all in good taste. They are very organized and particular when it comes to their clothes, and they are always spotlessly turned out. No-nos are clothes that look cheap or those that leave little to the imagination. Scorpios love that air of mystery. Well-known Scorpios are Vivien Leigh, Grace Kelly, and Burt Lancaster.

SAGITTARIUS

Frills and flounces don't turn Sagittarians on, unless of course they're being worn by someone Mr. Sagittarius is eyeing. They like clothes that adapt to the outdoor life that so many of them enjoy. Open-necked shirts and comfortable shorts please our male Fire sign, but if nagged into wearing something a little more dressed up, he'll pop for a well-cut blazer and slacks. Being active people, Sagittarians don't begrudge paying a lot for good sports clothes because they know it'll be money well spent.

Sagittarians often seem to go to extremes in their build and can be either very large or very small. There are many jockeys born under the sign of Sagittarius. Consequently, this sign has to be very fussy about its footwear, often having to get them handmade. Jeans are probably the favorite item of clothing in Sagittarius wardrobes, and they'll change things around by having plenty of attractive tops to go with them. A common hazard Sagittarians face is dog or cat hairs over their clothes—they can't resist patting animals. Clothes that are easily laundered are obviously necessary. Well-known Sagittarians are Liv Ullman, Frank Sinatra, and Dionne Warwick.

CAPRICORN

There's nothing Capricorns dislike more than standing out in a crowd. They prefer to blend in with the décor, and quite often their clothes detract rather than attract. Muted colors such as khaki, black, olive green, and blue/gray make up their basic wardrobe. They'll let their heads go a little with necklaces and earrings to add a bit of color to an otherwise somber outfit.

Male Capricorns are often found in professions that require conservative dress, so they can't really be blamed for not getting around in trendy gear. Ms. Capricorn really enjoys being a woman, and her clothes are feminine without being flashy. She likes blouses that are made of chiffon with long-flowing sleeves, and dresses that suggest, rather than broadcast, her womanhood. Don't expect to see your Capricorn wearing brief miniskirts or sporting ID bracelets or masses of jewelry. This is a very reserved sign as well as a thrifty one, and many a female Capricorn has been able to turn last year's outfit into this year's vogue for very little outlay. Famous Capricorns are Ava Gardner, James Earl Jones, Marlene Dietrich, and Danny Kaye.

AQUARIUS

Here is every designer's dream. The nonconformist Aquarian who loves nothing better than to keep up with fashion. Often Aquarians are so far out, they are in. This is the sign known as the Beautiful People and many of its members receive recognition as models and mannequins. Aquarians usually have long legs and a body that lends itself well to whatever garment they decide to drape around themselves.

Not all Aquarians show good fashion sense, however, and many Aquarian men still wear sandals with socks and pin-striped shirts with polka-dot ties. Some Aquarian women also look as though they grabbed the first thing out of the ironing pile and put it on. They like the space-age look and often opt for geometric hairstyles and off-beat colors. Silver and black together meets with their approval, as do lilac hues. Anything that sparkles or glitters for nighttime attire is a must, as for most Aquarians this is the time that they really come alive. Because they don't give a hoot what people think, they often spoil a nice outfit by wearing thongs or carrying a cheap purse. Well-known Aquarians are Mia Farrow, Carol Channing, Vanessa Redgrave, and Clark Gable.

PISCES

Ms. Pisces is the epitome of womanhood, and with the tools of the trade that she possesses—long eyelashes, feminine demeanor, and good figure—she is usually home safe when it comes to attracting the opposite sex. However, she doesn't leave anything to chance, and clothes are bought with one thing in mind: how to attract and catch the opposite sex. Dresses are made from soft clingy material, necklines are daring, and skirts and slacks are cut well to accentuate the curves.

The male Pisces is happy as long as he's got quality and comfort. He often sports a lot of jewelry, particularly Zodiac charms. He is ruled by the feet, so he's incredibly fussy about his footwear. There's nothing he likes more than to get back to nature in his off-duty hours, so comfortable beach clothes and leisure wear are high on his list of priorities. This sign is a romantic one, so glaring colors and ugly designs are rarely found in its wardrobes. As a matter of fact, most of Pisces' gear is impractical but lovely to look at. Favorite colors are turquoise, amethyst, black, and white. Most Pisceans would be wise to buy machine-washable garments because they attend many parties and are in constant demand for their company. Famous Pisceans are Elizabeth Taylor, Liza Minnelli, and Harry Belafonte.

FLOWERS AND
YOUR SIGN

Who hasn't at some time bought a bunch of flowers for a gift or as an apology? The old saying "say it with flowers" works even better if you can give someone the flower that is applicable to their own sign. These flowers don't necessarily have to grow in that particular sign's birth month; rather they tend to have the characteristics of that person, astrologically.

January is said to enjoy carnations and snowdrops. Carnations with their subtle perfume will appeal to Capricorns, as they dislike anything overdone. Snowdrops also rate well with their "pure as driven snow" morals.

February people enjoy the bright colors of the pansy and primrose. These don't grow too tall and are virtually work free, which appeals to the busy Aquarian. Great for hospital patients.

March is said to relate well to daffodils and violets. Elizabeth Taylor apparently loves the color purple and she's a Pisces.

April people love the color blue, so bluebells are a favorite with them. Their other flower is the daisy and the many varieties of the daisy family will suffice.

May is an "earthy" month and bulb-type flowers please Taureans. Lily of the valley and hyacinth head the list, but any flowers please them.

June weddings are often planned, and roses often form the basis of the bouquets. They are fairly adaptable to different climates, not so different from Geminis, who can live anywhere.

July can cover both Cancer and Leo, and it's interesting to note that the flowers associated with July are the water lily and the orchid. The exotic, sometimes temperamental, hothouse orchid sums up Leos very well.

August Gladioli and sunflowers both have bold colors and stand out in a crowd, a trait that is easily identifiable with August birthdays. Leos are ruled by the Sun so the sunflower pleases them.

September people love the multicolors of the aster and the calming blue of their other favorite, the delphinium.

October brings the sweet-smelling lilac and the pungent aroma of chrysanthemums. As Libra is a "sensory" sign, Librans much prefer the smell of a flower to the beauty of it.

November Sweet peas seem to grow well for the November birthday, as do gardenias and dahlias.

December Christmas bells, marigolds, and petunias with their bright happy little faces and hardy attitude reflect many Sagittarian characteristics.

FOOD
PREFERENCES

★

ARIES

If you want to impress Aries, don't do things by
halves. Take them out to the poshest restaurant
you can find and don't stint on anything, especially the tip. They love their food, and if it's
served with the minimum of fuss in elegant sur-
roundings, by people who really know their job,
they'll respect your judgment, and it'll be money
well spent in the long run. Their taste in food is
fairly simple; in the comfort of their own homes
they'll tuck into roast lamb, steak, meat loaf, veal
cutlets, and casseroles—not forgetting the chocolate cake, apple pie, and good old fruit salad and
ice cream. If you invite Aries around for dinner,
invest in a good bottle of brandy to serve with
their after-dinner coffee.

Diet Tips

Aries should avoid eating hot and spicy foods too often, as these make you thirsty, and the more you drink, the more likely you'll be plagued with fluid retention. Budget tip: lamb shanks. Special dinner: rack of lamb.

Favorite late night snack: grilled cheese and bacon sandwiches!

TAURUS

Food is a security blanket for Taureans, and this is why they have a constant battle with the bulge. It's not unusual to find the Bulls snacking on midnight feasts in the kitchen with the chair drawn up to the fridge. They have a sweet tooth and will forgo an entrée to make way for the dessert, if they are out to dinner. You can usually pick the Taureans, as they look at the sweets list on the menu before the main course. Fairly unadventurous with their cuisine, they pop for beef every time. The one stipulation here is that it must be well done. Very few Taureans like their steak still mooing as it's served up. They love their veggies, and they're not fussy whether they're cooked or raw as long as they look appetizing. Favorite sweets are apple pie, danish pastries, and strawberry shortcake.

Diet Tips

Bypass the rolls and skip the gravy. Special splurge dinner: roast beef and Yorkshire pudding.

Favorite quick dinner: spaghetti with a sauce made of anchovies, tuna, tomato pieces, parsley, and fresh ground pepper topped with Parmesan cheese.

GEMINI

Young Geminis love peanut butter and jelly sandwiches, but older people's tastes tend to be a little more subtle. The one good thing about taking Geminis out for lunch or dinner is that they usually insist on going dutch, so you can have a great nosh without using all the rent money. Chicken Chasseur, Duck L'Orange, marinated shish kebabs, rissoles, sweet and sour pork, or egg and chips will keep this Peter Pan of the Zodiac happy. Geminis lean to sweets that Mom used to make, like rice pudding, bread pudding, and homemade cakes. Romantic dinners should be accompanied by plenty of champagne cocktails.

Diet Tips

Weight isn't usually a problem here, rather the lack of it. Make your own milkshakes with bananas, strawberries, and a dollop of fresh cream.

The perfect Gemini binge: scrambled eggs on toast and Black Forest Cake, not necessarily in that order.

CANCER

When Cancerians are feeling low, they'll raid the fridge or bar, or both. Consequently they end up looking like their ruler, the Moon—round. They enjoy the flavor of herbs in cooking and they're the ones who polish off the herb or garlic bread at the restaurant before anyone else gets a look in. As Cancer is the home and family sign, Ms. Crab is great at turning budget-priced meats into gastronomic delights. Meat loaf, tasty stews, tuna Mornay, curried chicken and rice, lasagna, and homemade pizzas tempt flagging palates. Sweets are often baked apples, cheesecake, and coconut custard pie.

Diet Tips

Stop tasting the cooking while it's being prepared and cut down on dairy products and chocolate. Special occasion dinner: soft shell crabs.

LEO

Possibly the greatest hosts and hostesses of the Zodiac, so you can count yourself lucky if invited to dinner. Food will always be served piping hot and beautifully displayed. No expense is spared with the cuts of meat or the choice of wine. Leos have expensive tastes and like to try the more exotic meats such as venison or veal. They also lean toward things like tripe, brains, hearts, liv-ers, and kidneys. You can't really blame the king of the beasts for eating every scrap of the kill. Leos let their heads go over flambéed strawberries, rum raisin ice cream, and apple strudel. An extravagance they can't resist when dining out is dessert brought flaming to the table. At home they'll curl up like cats in front of the open fire, replete and happy.

Diet Tips

Lemon wedges with grilled fish and lots of salads will keep the body beautiful.

Best splurge: perfect lamb chops and asparagus with hollandaise.

VIRGO

Virgos are usually too busy helping others to become adept in the kitchen. Consequently, they find themselves becoming acquainted with a can opener at an early age. They are fussy with their food and critical of other people's attempts at cooking, driving the chef mad by inspecting everything to make sure it's clean. If they are forced to entertain, they prefer laid-back meals such as barbecues, fried chicken, fondues, Irish stews, and Welsh rarebit. Every now and again the Virgo goes on a health kick or decides to become vegetarian. Desserts Virgos like include frozen yogurt, sorbets, fresh fruit, and wonderful cheese plates. Naturally, if they are taken out, they have a field day with the menu, choosing the most expensive, exotic fare.

Diet Tips

Plenty of carrot and celery sticks, daily fiber intake, and a glass of hot water with a squeeze of lemon in it first thing in the morning.

Virgo passion: Chinese food, especially roast pork.

LIBRA

Libra loves to set the scene, so dinner parties are a sight for sore eyes with beautiful lace or embroidered tablecloths, sparkling crystal glasses, gleaming cutlery and elegant crockery. No table is complete without the stunning centerpiece usually arranged by this creative sign. As Libra comes under the sign of the "scales," it goes without saying that Librans have to keep their eyes on the pounds as they tend to creep on—more in the female sign, though, than the male. Usually very good cooks, they can change an ordinary dish into an exciting one with the adding of various herbs and spices. They enjoy veal dishes, subtle sauces, and easy-to-make, nourishing meals for the busy working Mom on the run. They love to pig out on petits fours or hand-dipped chocolates to round off a special dinner.

Diet Tips

Have entrée-sized main meals when dining out, and visit the powder room when the dessert menu comes around.

The perfect Libran diet meal: a plate of sliced fruit in season with a few pecans or walnuts sprinkled over it, topped with ricotta cheese. This provides the protein and calcium your diet needs without adding weight.

SCORPIO

This sign is sometimes referred to as "fire and ice," and the dishes Scorpios like often reflect this side of their nature. Piquant sauces, sweet and sour dishes, roast beef, steak Diane, caviar, smoked salmon, lemon chicken, chunky soups, and oysters Rockefeller are all favorites. Desserts tend to leave them cold, but if they're going to be tempted, they'll opt for lemon meringue pie, orange sorbet, Häagen-Dazs ice cream, and fruit pies. Adult Scorpios would happily skip the main meal and extend the happy hour, filling up on whisky sours, Cointreau on the rocks, or any other drink that comes their way. They like Chinese food and try to have it at least once a week. Favorites are Peking Duck, Mongolian Lamb, and Prawns.

Diet Tips

Make your own soups with chicken and fresh vegetables and grow your own lemon or grapefruit tree for a continual source of vitamin C.

Scorpio's favorite carbohydrate: Pasta al Fungi—or to the lay person, pasta with mushrooms in a creamy sauce.

SAGITTARIUS

Maybe it's because this sign is depicted as half horse, half human that Sagittarians go galloping around at breakneck pace and rarely have time to sit down to a leisurely meal. Hot dogs, hamburgers, and all kinds of deli sandwiches usually form part of their diet, so it's imperative that they eat at least one well-balanced meal per day. If they were dining out in an à la carte restaurant, they'd probably choose roast beef, rack of lamb, filet mignon, and flank steak, but at home they're just as happy with meat loaf, spaghetti Bolognese, grilled chops, rump roast, fish or cold meat, and salad. They'll usually smother the meat with an assortment of sauces or mustard. Any self-respecting Sagittarians, born under the "travel" sign, delight in foods from other countries, so at least once a month they'll visit a restaurant specializing in these dishes.

Diet Tips

Plenty of water, high-fiber cereal, and antacid tablets to relieve the constipation and heartburn all those rushed inadequate meals cause.

Sagittarians' best snack foods: fantastic pizzas and cheese-flavored popcorn.

CAPRICORN

This is the "banking" sign, so the housekeeping is worked out to the last cent. Ms. Capricorn is thrifty and likes her meals to be nutritious but not exorbitant in price, so she'll shop for weekly specials. She's great at keeping the cookie jar full of homemade treats and she makes a superb fruitcake. She finds a side of beef a good investment, as the Sunday roast is a tradition in this household and the other bits and pieces are turned into great stews. Capricorns really enjoy someone else paying for dinner, so they can really let their hair down and go all out. Lobster, crab, beef Wellington, steak Tartare, quail, trout amandine, or veal piccata would make their eyes light up and their mouths water, but children are just as happy with lasagna, ravioli, hot dogs, or bacon and eggs. Sweets that most Capricorns like include Cherries Jubilee, creme caramel, chocolate mousse, baked alaska, or ice cream sundaes.

Diet Tips

Not too many dumplings in the casseroles, and only small slices of cake without whipped cream. Fill the empty spots with plenty of fresh home-grown vegetables.

Second home for Capricorn: any Italian restaurant.

AQUARIUS

Wonderful zany, exciting Aquarians are the easiest sign to prepare food for. They dislike dull, stodgy people and loathe food that reflects them. Bland, uninteresting food bores them, and they're a boon for budding chefs who want to try out new taste sensations on them. Game to try anything once, it's this sign who'll taste snails, mahi-mahi, or tripe when no one else will. Watch Aquarius at a buffet: they'll pick up the hors d'oeuvres and dip them in anything that takes their fancy. Hot or cold, sweet or savory, it doesn't matter as long as it tickles the taste buds. They're innovative cooks and potluck means exactly that if you visit. They're just as happy with baked beans on toast, a bowl of cereal, or a toasted sandwich if they're slightly hungry after the theatre and will cook and eat in the finery they wore out. Sweets must be light and fluffy like zabaglione, homemade ice cream, apple cake, or chocolate éclairs.

Diet Tips

Being the "clotheshorse" of the Zodiac, you shouldn't have to worry about a diet, but just in case, whip up exotic fresh fruit cocktails in the kitchen blender.

The ideal Aquarian lunch for a lazy afternoon: poached eggs on toast and vegetables steamed with butter in the microwave.

PISCES

Pisces is the romantic. Soft lights, sweet music, and a loving companion will see Pisces swimming in the sea of tranquility. Pisces is classed as a "dual" sign as it's depicted by two symbols (the fishes). Pisceans aren't as one-eyed about seafood as the other two Water signs, Cancer and Scorpio; and in fact they prefer to compromise by having a seafood entrée followed by a meat dish. Pisces parents enjoy their children's parties as much as the young people and go to no end of trouble making fancy birthday cakes and unusual sandwiches. Animal lovers under this sign also ensure the pets have special tidbits now and again. Young lovers are happy dining out on the beach with hamburgers and french fries. Children enjoy McDonald's Fillet of Fish, tuna sandwiches, and hot dogs, while grown-ups delight in a lemon sole, chicken breasts, or tender steaks in a dimly lit floating restaurant. Any sort of dessert goes down well.

Diet Tips

Fish without the batter, lemon or vinegar instead of the salad dressing, and half a carafe of wine, not a full one, with the meal.

Pisceans' favorite entrée: beef cooked any way, braised, barbecued, grilled—you name it, they will enjoy it.

GAMBLING

★

It doesn't matter what star sign you are, each and every one of us at some time in our life has taken, or will take, a gamble. Let's look at how each sign copes with its gambling streak.

ARIES

Almost every type of sporting event has an Aries interested in it. This sign is often better fitted for gambling than the other signs because it can withstand a run of bad luck without displaying much emotion. Aries' recuperative powers are also very strong and they bounce back quickly for the next encounter. As the Arien nature favors consistency, they prefer to study the form of the horses or dogs before they place their hard-earned cash on them. This is borne out by my Aries brother, who has copies of *The Racing Form* crammed into his wallet and glove compartment, just in case the mood strikes when passing an OTB outlet. For special occasions such as the Kentucky Derby, or other big races, Ariens should follow the colors red and blue and names that suggest combat.

TAURUS

This practical sign doesn't like to part with its hard-earned cash, so unless something is "a sure thing," Taureans won't be tempted. They love animals, so they often go to the races just to watch, having worked out what they can afford to lose before they left home. Speculation should be avoided by Taureans, as they are notoriously short-sighted and would be better advised by a stock-broker. Copper or coal mining are stocks they should make money on and, of course, land. As an Earth sign they do very well buying or selling real estate. Lady Luck isn't very kind to this sign and the only way they're going to get good dividends from their investments is with cash in the bank and savings accounts. For that special "flutter," try names that suggest music or singing and the colors pink and green.

GEMINI

As long as Geminis' nerve holds out, they are cool gamblers. Unfortunately, the Geminian temperament means that they shift rapidly from one interest to another, expending all their time and money. If they stick rigidly to one venture and see it through to the bitter end, they'll probably break even. They have a retentive memory, and this is invaluable when they are following horses as they have total recall in their mind's eye of the last run and, even better, can pick a horse that was just barely beaten. The stock exchange stimulates them and provides a mental challenge, and the rapid buying and selling is right up their alley. However, because of the dual nature of this sign, Geminis can be millionaires one day and paupers the next. Colors to follow are white and yellow and names that suggest communication.

CANCER

This cautious sign doesn't need too many warnings as its motto could well be: "when in doubt, don't." Cancers can, however, get a long shot home every now and then just by the "feel" of the name. If they are out to make a bit of money, they tend to stick to the favorites, content to make minor headway instead of major loss. Problems can occur if they have a couple of beers before placing a bet and the brain becomes fuddled, or if they meet someone on the way to the window who talks them out of their choice. They are actually much better at handling other people's money and do very well wheeling and dealing with large companies or in banks where they're in charge of loans. As this sign is ruled by the stomach, horses whose names deal with food would be a good choice. Lucky colors should be blue/green.

LEO

A Leo regards speculation as part of his business and not a pastime. If there is a gamble to be taken, his interest is only maintained if he himself is able to take some part in bringing the venture to a successful conclusion. This therefore rules out many aspects of racing unless he or she is the owner/trainer. Leos also do well in gilt-edged securities, gold futures, and gold mining. They are bold, confident investors and make fewer mistakes than most people. When they do fall, however, they do it very heavily and get their fingers burned. They do better in large-scale enterprises and should stay away from small "flutters." Lucky bets will include horses with "gold" as a prefix or names that have a royal connotation. Colors to follow are orange and brown.

VIRGO

Like Leos, Virgos rarely do well in a ' flutter," but they do extremely well in systematically calculated gambles. All ventures should therefore be the product of patient study, and although the returns may be small, at least there'll be returns. Virgos will see through fly-by-night schemes, and if they decide to take on a business gamble, they'll want to examine the books from the last two years so they can calculate what the next five years' dividends will be. They can be real wet blankets if you take them along to the races, as they're always the first to say "I told you so" if your choice comes in a dismal last. The trouble is, they're usually right. For the intrepid Virgo, the best bet would be horses' or dogs' names that suggest communication and blue and white colors.

LIBRA

Libra is a dual sign, and Librans are literally two people when it comes to gambling. Either they go the whole hog and bet on anything that moves, or they invest their money in blue-chip stocks and wait for that investment to mature. If they belong to the former category, they should be able to stay on top as long as they use their own judgment and not others'. Librans are discriminating enough not to need the advice of colleagues and can make a good living in their own businesses. Horse trainers, entrepreneurs, publishing houses, and record companies often have Libras at the helm taking gambles; but because they have the happy knack of tuning into their intuition, these hunches usually pay off. Horses whose names suggest the law, music, or food usually pay off, as do the colors pink and brown.

SCORPIO

Very few Scorpios can resist the lure of cards or lotteries. They have reasonable luck but tend to overindulge. They face misfortune stoically, and their courage in the face of adversity is remarkable. If they have a Taurus or Capricorn partner, it can be a bone of contention if most of the paycheck goes into Lady Luck's pocket. This sign loves the hidden opportunity and enjoys ferreting out "the dark horse" of the field. Chances are this long shot will romp home, because who'd be silly enough to cross a Scorpio? Don't forget to repay a debt to Scorpio promptly, otherwise you can be sure you'll be paid back in kind, with interest. This sign is like the elephant—it never forgets. Best bets are names that deal with the occult and colors purple and black.

SAGITTARIUS

Sagittarians do well in sporting events as long as they are the competitors and not the bettors. They would get immense satisfaction out of being part of a syndicate that bets, but should only do this in moderation. Their love of animals, particularly horses, makes them excellent trainers or stud masters and this should be where their talents lie—in getting that particular animal to the race track and letting others invest in it. If this happy-go-lucky, Jupiter-ruled sign has a yen to part with a couple of dollars in a game of chance, it's better off with Lotto or the baseball pool, or maybe the occasional lottery ticket. Sagittarians are great to have around when only two legs of your trifecta get in, as this is par for the course with them. Special race days should see names that suggest travel, burnt orange, and black colors.

CAPRICORN

"A fool and his money are soon parted," mutters the Capricorn as you sail past him on the way to the betting window or Lotto counter. This canny Earth sign won't throw his or her money away on chance, preferring to invest in Mother Earth. Property, mining, and agriculture will soon see this person's bank balance growing. It's just as well Capricorns don't gamble much, as they would sink into excessive depression when things don't go their way. If you do take them to the races and blow your last dollar, they can be real Scrooges about lending you the bus or train fare. They strike a hard bargain when investing money, and their shrewd brains probably prompted the description "the banking sign." They'd probably do well as bookies, as I've yet to see one of them go broke. It's this sign that has one bet a year on the Belmont Stakes and wins. Capricorns should go for horses whose names suggest nature, and the colors beige and olive green.

AQUARIUS

Aquarians manage to land on their feet when everyone else has gone down, boots and all. They have the ability to plan a long way ahead and to be fortunate in deals that for anyone else would be dicey. They do extremely well in the backing of plays and rock concerts. They're not mad about animals and can live without the races, but they really enjoy poker, football betting, and Lotto. They have an "easy come, easy go" attitude and are great fun to have around. When they do win, you can be sure part of it'll go to someone who's been having a rough time. If pressed into choosing a horse on a big race day, they'll opt for lilac and white silks, and names that have an "offbeat" sound to them.

PISCES

Now here we have the sign that just adores to play the field. Horse or dog racing will draw Pisces like flies to the honey pot, and they'll not only bet on the favorite but also have a side bet on the underdog, hoping to get rich quick. This dream can often prove to be a nightmare for the long-suffering partners of Pisceans when the rent money goes on the backs of slow horses. Their best bet business-wise is to get into the import-export trade, oil shares, Marineland, or the local swimming pool, as these are more likely to give a return financially than the four-footed friends. Pisces' gullibility is their Achilles heel; they are easily taken in by a fast-talking salesman and many a sizable slice of Pisces' hard-earned savings has gone down the drain. Try names that denote water, and the colors gray and navy.

GIFT GIVING
BY THE STARS

★

ARIES

Any Aries will tell you the best gift of all is love. A simple hug or kiss is worth more than any diamond or mink jacket in Aries' book and, consequently, the more expensive presents get little or no reaction. This is a sign that loves to do things properly; Ariens don't know the meaning of half measures, so naturally, the giving and receiving of gifts is given the importance it deserves. Their natural reserve is reflected in their taste, so *please* don't buy them exotic lingerie, sex aids, gaudy clothes, or cheap jewelry or you may be one friend less.

Mr. Ram has a great sense of humor, so a Bill Cosby record or trick novelties for his bar would be appreciated, as would anything to enhance his car, like lambswool seat covers. Pure wool sweaters will keep his love light burning, and a game of chess should provide the mental warfare he enjoys so much.

Ms. Aries won't say no to pure wool blankets, silk scarves, linens, pottery, French perfume, and classical records. Just remember to leave the label on everything so she knows it's high class.

For our little lambs, dress-up outfits, toys that make loud noises like racing cars, fire engines, train sets, and space guns. Little girls will get hours of fun from dolls with long hair so that they can create hairdos, and stuffed toy animals. As this sign is ruled by the head, hair ribbons and colored barrettes are popular for girls while boys enjoy baseball caps or cowboy hats.

TAURUS

Taureans are givers more than receivers, so it's often difficult to pin them down about what they'd like. Being a very practical sign, Taureans tend to ask for useful things, when in fact, because they are Venus-ruled, secretly they'd adore something sensual.

Mr. Bull loves nothing more than to putter round his blooming garden in his spare time, so he'd really appreciate a load of topsoil to keep it this way. Garden tools will never go astray, nor would a new hose or flowering shrub (very practical).

For his social side, a new silk shirt or expensive after-shave lotion would make him "Bull of the Ball."

Ms. Taurus will be delighted with satin sheets, velvet scatter cushions, a new plant, the latest best-seller in the literary field, and birthstone jewelry.

Little Bulls love to use their hands, so building blocks, Play-Doh™, carpentry sets, and, because they are Daddy's little helpers, a toy wheelbarrow or lawn mower.

Miss Bull loves to play house, so toy brooms and dustpans, pretend kitchen utensils, and plenty of dolls keep her busy and happy. In her quieter moments or when she's confined to bed, painting and coloring books, modeling clay, and lots of reading matter will keep boredom at bay.

GEMINI

If you wondered where the saying "life wasn't meant to be easy" came from, it probably originated from those who've tried to buy something for the lovable, eccentric Gemini. Forget the more traditional gifts and search for something a little more out of the ordinary.

Mr. Gemini will get a kick out of adult games that keep his agile mind on the hop, so Trivial Pursuit, Pictionary, or backgammon will do for starters. Give him a ticket to a "mystery" weekend, or better still, a trip to Paris; with a bit of luck he might get the travel bug and stay out of your hair for a while. Air-conditioning for his car, a gift certificate for tapes and records, and also clothes will be appreciated.

For Ms. Gemini, handbags, cutlery, crystal glasses, and perfumed stationery will give pleasure; but remember when buying her clothes, the colors and line should be clear, bright, and uncluttered.

Master Gemini enjoys Junior Scrabble, Erector sets, Monopoly, pull-apart toys, and puzzles.

Little Miss Gemini would get hours of fun from a blackboard, dolls that talk, and when she's old enough, roller or ice skates. Young Geminis of both sexes are very musical, so a piano, accordion, guitar, or organ will give them hours of fun and parents a constant headache.

CANCER

This sign adores special occasions such as birthdays, Christmas, or anniversaries, as they allow Cancers to stuff themselves to their hearts' content without being told they are greedy. Edible gifts are enjoyed but often not worth the expense, as there's nothing to show within ten minutes of the gift being received. More practical for this home-loving sign are home appliances. Kitchen blenders, crock pots, and toaster ovens will please both male and female, as both are talented innovative cooks.

Mr. Crab loves water, so a new toy for his

swimming pool or liquid refreshment for his bar would be gladly accepted.

Ms. Cancer adores antiques, oil paintings, a new plant stand, bubble bath, or a bunch of flowers.

For young Cancerians the list is almost endless: flippers, snorkels, surf boards, bathing suits, sea-shell necklaces or earrings, Zodiac pendants, card games, new pets; and for the young teenager, waterproof watches, current Top 40 tapes or re-cords, or a Walkman.

LEO

Lordly Leos love buying for their loved ones, and they set out on a spending spree with scant thought for the budget. Consequently, when they give you your present, your own little offering pales in comparison. They don't want to show you up, it's just that they want their gift to be the biggest and the best.

The King of the Beasts' tastes run to the best, so one has to shop very carefully, making sure the gift shrieks with understated elegance. Leave the price tag on so he knows it cost you an arm and a leg. Gold chains that show off his broad chest and well-cut shirts that have a Gucci or Cardin label will bring a purr from this pampered pet.

Lionesses feel at home in fur coats, love to move in a swirl of exotic perfume, feel the cold, so electric blankets are gratefully received, while a makeup case with Lancôme makeup will certainly hit the spot.

Small Leos would enjoy a day at the Safari or zoo, stuffed animals of any shape, personalized mugs, new clothes, musical toys, baseball bats, tennis racquets, or rocking horses.

VIRGO

This sign's theme is "criticize and analyze," so it's no wonder people often shop for hours for Virgos' gifts, which usually end up as white elephants for the poor old Virgos. They really aren't a difficult sign to shop for as long as one remembers a few ground rules. Nothing in bad taste and it should have a useful function.

Males love video sets, tape recorders, calculators, stamp albums, watches, conservative clothes, or better still, a gift certificate, and a subscription to their favorite magazines.

Ms. Virgo loves a spotless kitchen, so small appliances or a new cookbook would be popular. Color-coordinated towels for her bathroom, perfumed stationery, lipstick or nail polish, and a new hair dryer wouldn't go astray. She's also a very nifty sewer, so a new sewing machine, if you can afford it, or an open order at a fabric shop will please her no end.

Young Virgos enjoy using their hands, so boys do well with model airplane kits, jigsaw puzzles, space games, and copper art kits. Little girls enjoy Spirograph, rug making, pick-up-sticks, Rubik's Cubes, and Crayola kits.

LIBRA

Home is where the heart is for Librans, so exchanging of gifts is usually at their place where they can excel in the job they shine at, playing host or hostess. As you wander around the living room, you'll notice every item is exquisitely molded and fits in beautifully with the decor. It's not a bad idea to ask Librans what they'd like, as they'd rather forgo the surprise than get something that is totally out of place.

Mr. Libra is a born flirt; clothes are a good choice. He's also very arty, so a good oil painting, tie, silver jewelry, or subscriptions to the opera or symphony orchestra will please his Venus-ruled nature. He often has a hobby that involves cars, so a radio-controlled car or plane would keep him occupied for hours.

Ms. Libra enjoys cooking, and a new set of kitchen scales or the latest saucepans would intrigue her. She also revels in being a woman, so bath oil, seductive lingerie, perfume, and beauty aids will be money well spent. Libra children are creative and like paint sets, sewing kits, macramé, bead threading, and packets of seeds for their own garden plot.

SCORPIO

Secretive Scorpios hate to admit it, but they love to receive presents. Anything that gets that mind of theirs ticking is enjoyed, so give plenty of thought to the gift before buying it.

Mr. Scorpio's love of mystery is catered to with spy or science fiction stories. The latest electronic gadgetry, golf clubs, a good bottle of wine, beach towel, fishing rod, or leather wallet are also good choices.

Ms. Scorpio enjoys mood music, tantalizing perfume, household linen, bath oils, black or red undies, a water bed, and a single red rose.

Most young male Scorpios enjoy chess games, chemistry sets, scuba gear, buckets and shovels, Rubik's Cubes. Little girls prefer ballet shoes, trampolines, bubble-blowing sets, and kaleidoscopes. As these young people spend a lot of time secreted away in their own little worlds (usually their bedrooms), bright colored posters make good presents.

SAGITTARIUS

This happy-go-lucky sign spends money like there's no tomorrow, so gifts are usually totally impractical and outrageously expensive. It doesn't matter though, as it's the thought that counts. Most Sagittarians have an interest in horses—if you can afford it, a part share in a race horse would be a dream come true for them. Less expensive would be an annual subscription to a racing magazine. For those who aren't interested in horses, any sporting equipment is fine.

Mr. Sagittarius would enjoy engraved beer or wine mugs, a cooler, a leather belt, a scarf in his favorite team's colors, video games, and maybe some new tires for the car.

She would love a portable TV set for the bedroom, a topaz ring, boots, a comfortable sweatshirt, a coffee maker, and someone to come in once a week to clean the house and do the ironing.

Master Sagittarius likes skateboards, scooters, minibikes, archery sets, dart boards, and any card game. Miss Sagittarius would like books, rocking horses, books about horses, china ornaments, roller skates, and jump ropes.

CAPRICORN

For Capricorns, Christmas comes right in the middle of their karmic cycle and their most demanding time. It's no wonder, then, that they find it hard to get inspired with the buying and giving of gifts. Birthdays aren't much better for them, as family and friends tend to combine both presents and it's the poor old Capricorn that gets short-changed on the gifts.

Mr. Goat would like new gardening gloves or tools, a lawn locker where he could keep everything neat and tidy, garden furniture, expensive tobacco if he's a pipe smoker. A new jacket will make you his Number One person.

Ms. Goat would enjoy a new tablecloth or place settings, an exquisite cut glass decanter or vase, a rug-making or tapestry set, pearls, and a sheepskin jacket. Stick with earthy colors if buying sweaters or linen.

Young Capricorns enjoy a wading pool, toys for the bath, piggy banks, boxing gloves, rubber stamps, and paint sets. Money tucked into a card will please them also.

AQUARIUS

What can you get for a spaced-out Aquarian who lives permanently on cloud nine and rarely bothers to come back down to earth? I admit it's not an easy task, but let's see if we can narrow the problem down.

The male Aquarian is like a peacock, loving to show off, so new clothes will see him preening his feathers. Remember to go to the trendy male shops and opt for outrageous designs. He likes to go to the races, so a stopwatch or new binoculars will be a hit. CB radios and the latest sound equipment are also safe bets.

Ms. Aquarius would like a new sewing machine, an extendable phone cord, a beautiful chiming clock, or a home computer.

Young master Aquarius loves space-age toys, a telescope or microscope, pinball machines, or mind-teaser games. Miss Aquarius will get a lot of pleasure from cutout dolls' clothes and doll house, a toy telephone, dolls that talk, snakes and ladders, and junior Trivial Pursuit. The whole Aquarian family would get a lot of use out of sleeping bags and a tent, as they love camping.

PISCES

Dreamy Pisces often have their hearts in the right place, but when it comes to practical gifts, they are sadly lacking in the know-how. One has to remember they are in love with love, so sentiment plays a strong part. They would rather have a gift given from the heart than one with an expensive price tag attached.

Mr. Pisces is a connoisseur and would appreciate a case of vintage wines, tickets to the ballet, the latest camera, or anything for his bar.

For her, a matching leather handbag and shoes, a pair of lambswool slippers, a crystal wine decanter, fresh flowers delivered every week, French perfume, and silk or satin shirts. Piscean children will enjoy a tropical fish tank, dominoes, photo albums, recorders, xylophones, soap on a rope, magic tricks, Yahtzee, magic sand, and face painting sets. This sign is away with the pixies most of its childhood, and Pisces children need very little to entertain them because they are masters of the art of make-believe.

HEALTH
PROBLEMS

ARIES

This sign is ruled by Mars, making it impetuous, impatient, and headstrong. It's no wonder, then, that Ariens' heads tend to be their vulnerable area. Tension headaches, migraine, neuralgia, sinusitis, impacted wisdom teeth, and balding are all familiar to an Aries. The young of this sign sport more black eyes and concussions than any other.

TAURUS

The ear, nose, and throat area pose problems here. Tonsillectomies, goiter and glandular troubles, middle ear infections, and head colds plague Taureans for most of their lives. Babies born under this sign nearly always get a heavy cold when teething, while young male adults often get a broken nose while playing sports.

GEMINI

Gemini rules the respiratory tract, the lungs, and the upper arms. Bronchitis, pleurisy, pneumonia, and asthma are a problem in the winter months with the probable exception of asthma which, in a young person, may be related to nerves or an allergy. Gemini people should keep their smoking to a minimum to give their lungs a chance.

CANCER

The breast and stomach belong to Cancer, and in women the breast checkup should be done regularly. When nervous or upset, Cancerian tummies will go through the butterflies they are so familiar with, and in extreme cases, this will often cause vomiting. Moms-to-be often suffer more with morning sickness, while ulcers are always a threat to the businessman. Preschool nerves will produce severe stomach cramps for some children.

LEO

Heart-related ailments will slow a Leo down. Leos should monitor their intake where rich foods are concerned, as cholesterol will build up quicker in this sign than in others. They feel the heat severely, and babies should be watched closely for heat exhaustion. They will often run fevers when teething, and young adults run the risk of sun-stroke after soaking up the sun for hours.

VIRGO

This sign is often referred to as the "salt of the earth," but privately I believe they should be called the "Epsom salts" of the earth. Virgos' sign is ruled by the intestinal area and they're forever flushing it out to keep their systems trouble-free. As long as they eat a well-balanced diet, they are relatively free from health problems.

LIBRA

Libra is ruled by the kidneys and also the nervous system. Nephritis, toxemia, edema, cystitis, and kidney stones are common complaints. Nervous breakdowns, shingles, and other nerve-related illnesses can make life miserable for this sign. It's important that Librans maintain a well-ordered life to keep their scales balanced.

SCORPIO

The lower trunk is the part most affected by health problems for Scorpios. This takes in the reproductive area and the hips. Women tend to suffer from painful menstrual periods or PMS while males can suffer from impotence, sciatica, sterility, nonspecific urethritis, and in later years, prostate problems. Broken hips or pelvis are likely to dog the Scorpio.

SAGITTARIUS

It's not surprising to find this athletic sign ruled by the muscular system. Cramps, torn tendons, and muscular dystrophy are some of the health problems encountered; but by and large, it's the superficial cuts, bruises, aches, and pains that come from pushing the body beyond its endurance that are par for the course with Sagittarians.

CAPRICORN

The bony parts of the body give Capricorn the most trouble. Gout, arthritis, rheumatism, tennis elbow, torn cartilage, and osteomyelitis are just a few of the problems common to this sign. Capricorns always know when it's going to rain as their hip joints tell them; and you can often pick this sign out by the telltale copper bracelet.

AQUARIUS

The lower limbs and spine are said to rule Aquarius. Lumbago, slipped discs, varicose veins, thrombosis, and whiplash are quite common. High or low blood pressure can also produce attacks of vertigo. Because they have no fear of heights, young people risk life and limb climbing trees and getting on roofs.

PISCES

As most Pisceans like a drink or three, the liver often takes a bit of a bashing. Other areas affected by this sign are the feet and ankles and the circulation. Most find it difficult to get warm and invest in bedsocks or hot water bottles. Ingrown toenails, bunions, and fallen arches are also prevalent.

HOME DECORATING

★

At some time or other, the urge to redecorate will overtake all of us whether we are newly married, jazzing up a work area, or just plain bored with the old style. Each sign of the Zodiac has its own taste and can be used effectively. Homes that have no shared taste in decorating often have problems within the relationship, and until harmony is restored, nothing blends together.

ARIES

The prerequisite for an Aries is usually expensive wool carpet. Ariens prefer to fork out their hard-earned cash on good quality floor fittings in neutral tones and then go to town on the rest of the color scheme. The male Aries is fairly dominant, so he won't take too kindly to frills or wishy-washy colors, particularly in the bedroom, where he loves to be boss. Living room suites are often leather, deep and comfortable. Aries would prefer to wait longer and buy the best than to fill the house with cheap imitations. The kitchen will be spotless and have touches of orange throughout, and many an Aries house has an indoor/outdoor room where people can relax and have a few drinks.

Aries children can be quiet and introverted at times, so their bedrooms should be bright and comfortable. Boys often have bedspreads with vintage cars on them, but little girls may enjoy frills and flounces with lots of blue. A space heater will ensure this Fire sign will be warm on the coldest days.

TAURUS

This earthy sign is happy as long as her plants are, and it's a full-time job just to keep them that way. She is a good housekeeper, but only because she's well organized. Easy-care fabrics and functional furniture are her choice, and you can forget about the venetian blinds unless they are self-cleaning. Chocolate-brown sofas in velvet with pale blue satin scatter cushions appeal to Taurus and, of course, the obligatory potted plants. There's usually a feeling of homeliness in a Taurus household. Rooms have a "lived in" look and comfort is the main theme. Feature walls are often wood panelling or brick, and there are plenty of chrome and glass fittings around. Bedrooms have a no-nonsense décor, probably reflecting what goes on in there.

Children born under the sign of Taurus need plenty of bookshelves and, if possible, a window overlooking a garden so they can tune in to nature.

GEMINI

This sign is probably the best natural interior decorator of the Zodiac. Gemini's uncanny ability to mix and match colors can produce mind-boggling results and every room manages to give you a lift. Plenty of white is the mainstay of the color scheme, and lots of windows to let in light and fresh air. As this is a "communicative" sign, the living room is Gemini's favorite place to relax. Modular living room furniture, plenty of subdued lighting, and good music will keep any party going and have guests coming back for more. Like the other Air signs, the outdoor entertainment area is very attractive, with comfortable leisure furniture and cool shaded areas.

Children's rooms are usually a kaleidoscope of color with brightly painted bunks and boldly patterned furnishings. It's a good idea to cover a section of the wall with a blackboard so this "writing" sign can scribble to its heart's content.

CANCER

A peaceful existence is all a Cancerian craves, so rooms have to be decorated in cool muted colors, and furniture should blend and not offend the senses. This sign loves antiques and will often decorate a room around one piece of furniture. The two favorite rooms are likely to be the bathroom and kitchen. The bathroom should be large, with plenty of shelf space for bath oils and aftershaves. Large, colorful fluffy towels entice visitors to sink into a scented bath after a long journey. Since they are innovative, rather than good cooks, the kitchen should house a walk-in pantry with lots of cookbooks for Cancer to try out new recipes on unsuspecting family members.

Nurseries and toddlers' rooms are usually filled to overflowing with stuffed toys, while teenagers' rooms look like the local dump and are a mother's nightmare. Color schemes are often aquamarine to remind them of the sea and gold for the sand.

LEO

Every lion and lioness feels at home in the den and the human species of Leo isn't very different. Dad will often use this room as a retreat and will decorate it in the warm vibrant colors of brown, gold, orange, and black. Ms. Leo may turn it into her sewing room, opting still for the warm sunny colors but breaking them down with beige. Like all Fire signs, Leos hate the cold, so heating has to be efficient. Many choose solar heating for pools and hot water systems. This is an extravagant sign, and Leos' furnishings are the biggest and the best. You don't see this family trying to keep up with the Joneses—they *are* the Joneses. They have excellent taste in art, and bold bright paintings lift the living room and dining area. It's not unusual to see an animal skin decorating the floor in front of an open fire. It brings out the hunter in them.

Baby cubs will lie quite happily in their crib or bassinet if there is a large mobile in the shape and color of the sun swinging gently overhead. They will fret if the room is decorated in somber colors.

VIRGO

This studious sign needs peace and privacy, as many Virgos are students and therefore need a corner of the house where they can get away from it all. A study should be decorated in colors of light blue and navy, with touches of white. Built-in bookshelves, a large desk, good desk lamp, and plenty of electrical outlets are essential as this sign does a lot of taping and computer work. A Virgo's bedroom can be quite austere, with few frills and flounces but plenty of drawer and closet space for their clothes. Ferns or African violets will brighten up the décor.

Children's rooms are very practical, with built-in bunks and desks decorated in natural wood. A large wastepaper basket would be a good investment and large hooks to hang clothes on, as they tend to hang on the floor otherwise.

LIBRA

Lots of space, clean lines, and fresh air is what Librans look for when decorating. Balance this out with plenty of plants and they're content. Black and white can be found in the male Libra's favorite room, but Ms. Libra runs to softer colors. One of the rooms, possibly the bedroom, will be decorated in pale apricot or salmon colors with attractive bedside lamps and frilly curtains and covers. Kitchens will be functional with lots of copper to brighten them up. Blue, green, and brown are often the colors chosen for this room.

Libra children love pictures, so a plain wall can be highlighted with a corkboard to display their artistic efforts. Washable paint is preferable to wallpaper as this sign loves playing with modeling clay; and carpet sprayed with Scotchgard will save time and temper when parents have to clean up afterwards.

SCORPIO

If Scorpios are able to design their homes, they'll always include a sunken living room or a cellar for their vintage wines. They are night owls, so this particular room should be well away from the rest of the house so as not to disturb the others.

Scorpios are a little intolerant, so it might be wise while the children are small to invest in hard-wearing, rather than attractive, furniture. Later on, they can invest in the expensive stuff. They are usually very handy around the house, but partners would be wise to move out of earshot, as the language can get very colorful. As Scorpio is a Water sign, quite a lot of time will be spent in the bathroom, so a spa bath or Jacuzzi would be a worthwhile investment.

A teenage Scorpio will probably want a water bed and purple and black color schemes; they'll be quite happy with bean bags to sit on.

SAGITTARIUS

Carpet and furniture that doesn't show dirty paw marks or cat hairs is usually the first thought that enters Sagittarians' minds when redecorating. Not for them the antique furniture or feminine décor; they don't have the time or inclination to keep it that way. As far as they're concerned, a house is meant to be lived in, not to be a showplace. Their pride and joy is often a rumpus room where a pool table, bar, dart board, and battered old stereo offer many relaxing hours. Exposed beams, natural wood walls, and chocolate-brown, red or orange, and sunny yellow cushions make this a delightful, relaxing room.

There's often an exercise bike tucked away in the corner of the adults' bedroom, while youngsters need plenty of shelf space for roller skates, tennis racquets, and footballs. A rocking horse would be a worthwhile investment for the nursery.

CAPRICORN

This home usually reeks of good taste. Everything is understated, and furniture and furnishings are chosen for durability. Favorite colors are usually olive green, rust, brown, and beige, and this is carried right through the house. Capricorns enjoy washing and ironing, so a large laundry is necessary. Quarry tiles are a favorite and found in laundries and sunrooms. Their garden is very important, and this is where their imagination runs riot with colors they wouldn't use in the house. It's almost as though the house restricts their decorating ability.

Children's rooms are decorated lovingly with prints that coordinate with the theme; curtains and bedspreads are often handmade. Like every other room of the house, not a thing is out of place. Capricorns are very clever with their hands, and cushion covers or small mats and often patchwork quilts will take pride of place in a teenage bedroom.

AQUARIUS

This sign is usually very untidy or extremely meticulous. If you try to regain order in the house of an untidy Aquarian, you will find it a lost cause.

Multicolored piles of ironing vie with the existing color scheme, and chairs will look two-tone due to various garments draped over them. Both types love blue, white, silver, gray, and mauve, and if you visit the well-ordered Aquarian's house, it can be a very pleasant experience. Problems can arise in the disorganized Aquarian household when boredom sets in during wallpapering or renovating. It remains half-done for months or until a Virgo or Aries finishes it.

Teenagers' rooms are like visiting another planet, with all the space-age technology they manage to amass. Babies need sturdy furniture that they can climb on without too much damage.

PISCES

Gentle dreamy Pisceans create another world within their four walls. Often the living room is dominated by a tropical fish tank, and subdued wall lighting creates a relaxing effect. There's usually a bowl of fresh flowers on the table. The smallest room in the house doesn't get overlooked and often has zany wallpaper in it. There are no jarring colors, garish modern furniture, or bad paintings in the rest of the house. Their one luxury will be an expensive sound system and teak wall buffets and bars. They love playing host or hostess, so a dining room will be color-coordinated right down to napkins, crockery, and place mats.

Children's bedrooms should be decorated in gray,

lilac, and burgundy colors broken up with white. A natural pine bunk or bed will blend well. As most young Pisceans suffer from nightmares, a night-light is a must, plus a bowl of goldfish.

MONEY
MANAGERS OF
THE ZODIAC

ARIES

If you have an Aries bank manager or accountant, one thing you can be sure of is that your account will be run with military efficiency, total dedication, and no excuses if you sneak into the red. This is all very commendable when Ariens are handling other people's money, and it's all there in black and white; but when it comes to practicing what they preach, the gremlins sneak in and foul up the works. The budget will go according to plan until Ms. Aries spies a bargain or heads off to the seasonal sales. He's no better, as he's an easy touch when it comes to cars or sporting equipment. Somehow between the cash in hand and the writing of the deposit slip, the best-laid plans will go astray.

TAURUS

Taurus is often called the "banking" sign, and this is borne out by the number of Taureans who choose to make their careers in banking, insurance, and accountancy. Children who have Taurean parents often have healthy bank accounts by the time they leave school, but the ever-watchful eye of Mr. or Ms. Bull will squelch any ideas of having a great bash and spending the lot. Older Taureans can be superbores when they constantly tell their children how they scrimped and saved for them. By all means ask a Taurean for a loan; they'll give it gladly as long as you don't mind repaying with interest. If you really want to be devious, watch Taureans do battle with their conscience when they are offered a bargain in oil paintings, crystal and china, or some other temptation.

GEMINI

Geminis unintentionally cause more gray hairs for bank managers than any other sign. It's not that they don't want to part with their hard-earned cash; it's just that they never seem to find time to fill in the deposit slip correctly. It's no good taking Geminis at their word. Of course they'll pay the loan back on payday—but to make sure, you'd better be waiting with your hand outstretched the minute they receive it. On the other hand, they are great to borrow from because they may not get around to collecting it for six months. Go into a

Gemini's home and you'll see where all the money goes. Video equipment, expensive sound systems, and all the latest records promise the greatest parties on the street.

CANCER

"A fool and his money are soon parted," says the old adage, and I wonder if the person who penned it was a Cancerian or perhaps knew one. No magic act can compete with the deft way this sign has of making money disappear; and what's more, Cancerians honestly won't know where it went. We could hazard a guess and say a large proportion would go on eating, drinking, and making merry. There's also the impractical, but oh, so lovable side of this person who borrows off his mother and then spends three quarters of the loan on a bunch of flowers or expensive box of chocolates to say thank you. Cancerians live beyond their means, having champagne tastes on beer salaries, but when they are "flush," the lucky ones they love will get the benefit.

LEO

"Biggest and best" is Leos' motto and they'll work hard to achieve this. Money or the lack of it can cause a premature state of anxiety in this sign, so it's not unusual to see a Lion or Lioness holding down two jobs to keep themselves in the luxury they'd like to be accustomed to. Most of the paycheck goes on their backs and to the hairdresser, and hang any other little incidentals such as food, rent, or mortgage repayments. They reckon clothes maketh the man/woman, and as long as they look the part, they should land well-paid jobs or rich spouses. In partnership with Leos, don't make the mistake of letting them handle the housekeeping if it's a biweekly paycheck. You'll eat like kings the first week and paupers the second.

VIRGO

Cool, calculating Virgos know right down to the last cent where their money goes. They spend hours over the bank statement and are a supermarket checkout operator's nightmare. Every item is double-checked, leaving no room for error, and bills are paid with a promptness that has the recipient a little suspicious. Debt is a dirty word and loans are frowned upon. Bank tellers love the Virgo who does the banking. Every note is arranged end-to-end in true banking order and neatly secured with rubber bands. This is the sign that saves for a rainy day, but it never rains hard enough to draw it out. One weakness might be an overseas vacation, but Virgos will wait until it's the "off season" to save money.

LIBRA

Now you see it, now you don't, seems to be the watchword of Libras regarding their finances. They spend months saving hard until they've got a healthy bank balance and a bit of security, but when the spirit moves them, they'll blow the lot with no remorse. Fast cars, boats, expensive jewelry keep this sign close to the borderline. Libras try extremely hard to balance the budget, as their symbol, "the scales," would predict, but somehow or other this juggling act is usually a fizzer. Mr. Libra spends a lot of his budget socializing, while Ms. Libra loves good food, designer clothes, and expensive makeup. When dating, they'll often insist on going dutch, as this appeals to their sense of fair play.

SCORPIO

Never make the mistake of trying to pull a fast one on a Scorpio. It's no good saying there was no change if he or she sends you out on an errand. They will have tabulated the cost down to the last percentage of the cent. Scorpios are endowed with computers instead of brains, so nothing gets past them, least of all the intricacies of the dollar. This is the sign that writes everything in the budget book and sets one night a month aside for the auditing of the partner's bank statements. Loans that are required from this person, no matter whether it's one dollar or one hundred, should be set out in writing, preferably in triplicate, with the required seven days' waiting period.

SAGITTARIUS

Sagittarian males should offer up heartfelt thanks to the Sagittarian women because without them we would probably see their extinction. If it was left to the males, the only people to benefit from their generosity would be the races, clubs, and the neighborhood sports bar. Ms. Sagittarius is born with a built-in survival kit, and she soon has her priorities worked out. She enjoys a drink and a bet as much as her male counterpart, but not until *after* she has worked out her budget. Animals are Sagittarians' weak spots and a good amount of money can be spent on them, particularly if they work in their breeding and training, but then the money is well invested.

CAPRICORN

When a Capricorn opens up the purse or wallet, the moths fly out. This is *the* sign of the Zodiac that knows all about Mr. Scrooge. Now, before I get attacked on all sides by irate Capricorns, I hasten to add that they are not miserly, just careful. What other children could bank their pocket money and then charmingly use everyone else's? What other sign (apart from Virgo) has a nervous breakdown at the mere thought of drawing money out of the account for a new dining table while there is still life in the old? What Capricorn woman doesn't fret when the bills come in? One good thing: you'll never meet a debt collector if you're married to a Capricorn.

AQUARIUS

This sign is a supreme worry; it travels in the fast lane the moment it arrives on this planet. Aquarians live for today, and let tomorrow take care of itself because, as they reason, you can't take it with you. Lifestyles aren't important to them, and they'll adapt to whatever environment they find themselves in. They are a fairly intuitive sign and can often make quick killings on the stock market. They are thrill seekers, and they can take off on a trip at a moment's notice, with or without finances to back them. Most of a paycheck will go on computer games, pinball machines, telescopes, or dress materials. Partners will have to play the heavy and recoup loans because the Aquarian won't.

PISCES

This sign always has the best intentions, but unfortunately, they don't often come to fruition. Don't send Pisceans down the street to buy inexpensive dishes or they'll come back with Royal Doulton bought on time. Now and again you can come across a practical Pisces, but they are as scarce as hens' teeth, so don't hold your breath. They are great at buying presents for special occasions but not at remembering to pay fines, car registration, or health insurance.

NAME DAYS

★

Monday's child is fair of face,

Tuesday's child is full of grace,

Wednesday's child is full of woe,

Thursday's child has far to go,

Friday's child is loving and giving,

Saturday's child works hard for its living,

But . . . the child that is born on the Sabbath day
is bonny, blithe, good, and gay.

MONDAY'S CHILD

Monday is taken from the Old English word
Monandaeg, and literally translated means Moon
Day. It can be said that the Monday birthday

people are fair of face and fair with their judgment of others. Emotions often run high with this person, and things can be said but not meant in the heat of the moment. They feel things very acutely, hence the old saying "mooning" around when suffering the pangs of unrequited love. Mondayitis is often more pronounced with Monday people, and they find it harder to get going.

Love

Falling in and out of love is an occupational hazard, and it's not uncommon to see Monday's children experience more than one marriage in a lifetime. They love to flirt, being blessed with good looks that make the job easier. Unfortunately, they tend to look at life through rose-colored glasses, and this view brings them back to earth with a bump more often than not.

Career

Anything that brings out their creative talents should be encouraged, and photography, interior design, architecture, à la carte cooking would all produce good results. They have a good sixth sense when it comes to the crunch and should rely on this when in doubt. Astrology and clairvoyance could also be taken up as professions.

Travel

Restlessness is never very far beneath the surface here. They love to have a mental challenge and enjoy being on the go, whether with business or pleasure. Many have a checkered early life, brought about by frequent moves due to a parent's job. They prefer to save for years and have one big holiday with all the trimmings than to cut corners and take a few short ones. Although they like to be independent, home is always where the heart is for Monday's child.

Finance

Monday people love money. If they aren't born into it, they'll start at an early age, selling papers, running errands, or mowing lawns to build up their bank account. Once they get a few dollars behind them, they use this as their springboard to self-employment and are mini-tycoons by about thirty. They always save for a rainy day and often have the first dollar they earned framed over the mantelpiece.

Home and Family

Those born on Monday usually make strict but fair parents. They find it hard to show affection but will always listen to both sides of a story. Their down-to-earth attitude makes them a favorite with other members of the family, and they're aways ready to share a "cuppa" with a good dollop of sympathy. Their home is usually of solid construction and never short of visitors. Monday people make excellent hosts and hostesses.

TUESDAY'S CHILD

"Full of grace," as the saying goes. Tuesday comes from the Old English word *Tiwesdaeg*, which literally translated means "Day of Tiw," representing the Latin "Dies Martis"—Day of Mars. In astrology, Mars is the war god and is full of fire and action. Combine this with grace and you've got someone who is light on his or her feet, not afraid of hard work, and a certain champion of the underdog. Quick to fire, Tuesday people often act first and have to make amends later.

Love

Tuesday people love fiercely and at times impractically through their flights of fancy and impetuous actions. Romantic upheavals upset them for years, and they often hang on to relationships even though the fire in them has long gone out. They are very moral people, and once committed to something or someone, they'll see it through until the bitter end. It's all or nothing with them, and they'll often start an argument because they love to kiss and make up.

Career

Government institutions have their fair share of Tuesday people working for them, particularly the armed forces, the police force, nursing, teaching, and politics. People born on this day are usually musically inclined and have the stamina to do well in gymnastics or professional sports. They do prefer to be their own bosses and work well without supervision.

Travel

Tuesday people often exchange countries, and many a migrant will find they were born on this day. Travel for these people is usually in answer to an SOS or because their job requires it for promotion of their own talents, like author tours or to publicize a record. The early part of a Tuesday childhood is often spent traveling between two homes as a result of parents' divorces.

Finance

These are the givers and not the receivers, because money isn't that important to them and they'd rather give it to a worthy cause. Once they establish a steady income, they'll let the more ambitious pass them in the career stakes. Their motto could well be "you can't take it with you."

Home and Family

Overprotective of their loved ones, the Tuesday people can make the mistake of smothering their families. Teenagers often rebel against the strict regime and fiery exchanges that are the order of the day in the Tuesday parent. Strong family ties, however, cement strong bonds that last throughout life, often with a religious upbringing. Any weddings planned by a Tuesday person will be a large-scale production with no expense spared.

WEDNESDAY'S CHILD

Who would want a Wednesday child when they're supposed to be full of woe? This is in fact a fallacy, because the word is derived from the Old English *Wodnesdaeg* or "Woden's Day." The Latin translation is "Mercurii Dies," or Mercury's day. Mercury-ruled people are far from "woeful," in fact they can be the biggest practical jokers; they love to have the floor; and they flit from person to person or job to job like bright butterflies. They are versatile, clever, and communicative, steering clear of moody, reserved people.

Love

Wednesday's children have more ups and downs in love than a roller coaster. They seem to have spates of emotional turmoil that come in waves, and their personal life is far from dull. They need a stable partner who can provide an anchor for them. When hurt or upset, a Wednesday person can retreat into moody silences or charge the air with verbal assaults—there are no half measures.

Career

Being busy little bees with a nose for sniffing out a good story, it's no wonder the Wednesday person makes a great journalist or detective. There's very little that Wednesday people can't turn their hands to, and they excel in hairdressing, jewelry design, acting, engineering, and entertainment. They thrive on activity and will work their butts off until boredom sets in.

Travel

Mental travel rather than physical travel appeals to this person. They love to dream of holidays on a grand scale without ever leaving terra firma. These flights of fancy are certainly a lot cheaper than the real thing. If given a choice, they'll choose short periods of actual travel, as they go stir-crazy being cooped up in small places like the cabins of ships or planes for any length of time. Mountaineering or hang gliding would appeal to their sense of adventure.

Finance

Easy come, easy go is the Wednesday code. Although by no means a fall guy when it comes to the dollars and cents, Wednesday people have a philosophical point of view regarding finance. Their agile minds can balance a budget in no time flat, but they never check their change to see if it's correct. Interestingly enough, the Wednesday charmer never ever seems to be flat broke, but at the same time will never be a millionaire. All in all, Wednesday's children manage very well.

Home and Family

Without meaning to, Wednesday children often transfer the woe to another person. They are fairly restless characters, and parents often lose their children as young adults, when the call of the wild beckons them and they go out to tackle life. Once married, they often move interstate or overseas, again causing parents' tears. Once the wanderlust has been sated, they will settle down to being loving parents and doting grandparents.

THURSDAY'S CHILD

Who wouldn't have far to go with Thor the thunder god wielding his hammer over your head? The word Thursday, from the Old English *Thursdaeg*, literally means "Thor's Day." People born on this day often have a lot to say, most of the time loudly. They can be a force to be reckoned with, even if they aren't the loud bullying type, as they walk softly but carry a big stick. They have the ability to analyze and compute, often disconcerting others with their astuteness. True friends or formidable enemies—you either love or hate a Thursday person.

Love

Difficulties will often arise because of the high standards set by this person; they strive for perfection and expect the same in return. They put loved ones on pedestals only to find they have clay feet. Mixed marriages are quite common, as Thursday people don't worry about race or creed, and they're champions of the underdog. You may capture them physically, but you'll never harness them mentally.

Career

As long as Thursday people are working with people en masse, they are happy. Social welfare, religious callings, medicine, scientific work, engineering, computer technology, or the police force are all worthwhile careers for them. They usually rise very rapidly through the work ranks to positions of seniority and responsibility.

Travel

The less-developed countries often draw these people to them like a magnet. Communes also interest them, and single young adults born on Thursday often set off around the world on a shoestring budget, much to their parents' dismay. Their interest in how the other half lives shows in their preference for working holidays or exchange student programs. They are quite willing to rough it, if necessary, and are great companions on camping trips.

Finance

Woe betide the partner or family member that blows the budget. That's when the Thursday child rumbles and looks as bleak as thunder. A place for everything and everything in its place applies especially to the checkbook, and there's no way you can beat this computer brain when it comes to dollars and cents. Thursday people make good investments and rarely waste money on things that don't have a good financial return. If you borrow money from them, be prepared to pay it back with interest.

Home and Family

Tireless workers for home and family, the Thursday parents provide a stable and loving framework for their family to live and grow in. Mr.

Thursday is usually a workaholic, and although he brings home a good paycheck, he often has a second job. As a result, it usually falls upon Ms. Thursday to rule the roost, a job she does admirably. Children return to the home time and time again, long after they're adult, enjoying the harmony and stability they've grown up with.

FRIDAY'S CHILD

Friday is taken from the Old Engish word *Frigdaeg*, or more literally "Freya's Day." Freya, according to Norse mythology, was the goddess of love and fecundity, sister of Frey who was the god of Earth's fertility and dispenser of prosperity. The old nursery rhyme has Friday's children as "loving and giving" and this seems to be true, because they are suckers for a sad story and will give away their last dollar to a needy cause. People find it easy to off-load their problems on them, as they are envied for their ability to stay cool in a crisis.

Love

As the name Freya suggests, love is as necessary to a Friday person as eating and breathing. The girls are born charmers and from an early age have Dad wrapped around their little fingers, while the males have a magnetism that the girls find hard to resist. Their hearts definitely rule their heads and, as a result, long-term relationships can be a problem until all their wild oats have been sown. Both sexes revel in the attraction they hold for the opposite sex, but promiscuity is a no-no.

Career

These people have their heads screwed on the right way when it comes to business. They drive a hard bargain and won't take or give any quarter. Insurance, banking, real estate, show business, catering, animal breeding and training, all bring worthwhile results. They prefer jobs that have them working outside or that have a constant flow of people around them.

Travel

People born on Friday like to put firm roots down as early as possible, and consequently, most of their travel is done in the early or later years of life. Reminders of their trips are their "objets d'art" that take pride of place in the living room. They are sentimentalists at heart and old photos, mementos, and home movies are often brought out as nostalgic reminders of the good times they had.

Finance

Prosperity may be just a pipe dream for Friday people, but they are rich in things other than material assets. Whatever they acquire comes from sheer hard work and even this may elude them until after thirty-five. They'll usually find the middle road brings self-satisfaction. As the old saying goes: "All good things come to those who wait," and the loving and giving attitude of a Friday person guarantees this.

Home and Family

Friday people often come from large families, or once they're married, they produce offspring at an alarming rate. Friday women are content to be wives and mothers. Green fingers are not uncommon among them, and the garden blooms as a result. They enjoy people, and a Friday-born host or hostess gives great parties. Friday teenagers seem to draw the crowd to their place, much to the consternation of parents.

SATURDAY'S CHILD

Saturday is the seventh and last day of the week and the Jewish Sabbath. The old English name, *Saeternes Daeg*, is the translation of the Latin "Saturni Dies" or Day of Saturn. Saturn was the Roman god of agriculture and vegetation, so it's not surprising that people tend to get out in the garden on Saturday. Saturnalia is also known as a period of wild revelry, and we all know how to let our hair down and unwind on Saturday nights. Those born on a Saturday probably work harder and play harder than those born on the other days.

Love

Those born on Saturday often have two sides to their natures. Extroverted in their personalities, they are often quite introverted emotionally and find it difficult to commit themselves totally to a personal relationship. Very often they remain single until quite late in life, preferring to answer to no one but themselves until they are sure of total commitment. Once married, they like to maintain a certain amount of physical and mental freedom or they chafe at the bit.

Career

Saturday's children work hard for a living, and no one knows it better than they. Hard physical work seems to draw them like a magnet and many stonemasons, bricklayers, construction workers, landscape gardeners, nurses, stage workers, furniture movers, and butchers are Saturday people.

Travel

Traveling from site to site, or location to location, keeps them on the go. Many of them have careers in the armed forces, so they get to see the world while they're working, getting the best of two worlds. When they find time to relax and travel for pleasure, it has to be first class all the way. Most trips are planned with military precision, and it's rare to find anything left behind or not done. Young people often have pen pals from all over the world because they make friends easily.

Finance

Saturday people and Monday people should get together in business because they both like to use other people's money. Saturday's child saves his or her pocket money and manages to put the bite on other family members in the nicest possible way. Self-made millionaires often come under the Saturday birthday, but it's usually through holding down a couple of jobs and working darn hard. Young people tend to blow all the money they've saved on impractical and extravagant items, but they still manage to keep the wolf from the door.

Home and Family

Family ties are very strong here and children are brought up to respect their elders. Family discussions are encouraged and major decisions are made only after everyone has had his say. Family outings always include grandma, a neighbor, or the family pet. The motto is usually "troubles shared are troubles halved." Very private people, they don't air their dirty linen in public and make excellent neighbors and loyal friends. When in need, turn to a Saturday person; they won't let you down.

SUNDAY'S CHILD

According to the rhyme, Sunday's child gets all the good things rolled into one. Bonny, blythe, good, and gay—so it's well worth waiting for. The word Sunday comes from the Old English *Sunnandaeg*, the translation of the Latin "Dies Solis" or day of the sun. It is the Christian day of worship. Most people relax and enjoy themselves on this day of the week, content to renew family ties and forget the material side of life. Those who have this birthday seem to have an enormous capacity for charitable work.

Love

Love for one's fellow man is all important to Sunday people. They are the givers and not the receivers and often devote their life to religious callings. They are rather gullible and will swallow an old line time and time again. They rarely see faults in others and, because of this, tend to learn the hard way in love. Their partners have to learn to take second place to whatever charitable cause they take up. They can be aloof and undemonstrative, but this doesn't mean they don't feel very deeply.

Career

The obvious choice for a Sunday birthday is religion, followed by social welfare, kindergarten teaching, any form of entertainment, floral art, cake decorating, beautician or cosmetician work, airline careers, or TV production. As long as there is the feeling of a job well done, this is payment enough.

Travel

Sunday's children begin musical houses at an early age. Each move is a little more substantial than the last, and by the time they are teenagers, many miles have been put between them and their birthplace. Relations are usually scattered all over the world, so this necessitates long-distance travel when engagements or marriages take place. Sunday people often travel in groups, preferring the hustle and bustle of crowds to being alone.

Finance

Any donations are gratefully received by Sunday's children because they often have trouble making ends meet. They aren't great gamblers and most of their windfalls come through the intervention of others. Settlements and legacies or lottery tickets given to them for birthdays often put them on their feet. They should never lend money or buy beyond their means. The fine print on documents should always be read or pointed out to them before they sign on the dotted line. The Sunday person is a salesman's dream.

Home and Family

"The family that prays together stays together" could be the motto of the Sunday birthday. Even when the family is scattered, constant communication is kept up and, for many, the Sunday church service is strongly adhered do. This can sometimes have an adverse effect on strong-willed young adults who will go to the opposite extreme to get off the straight and narrow, often with dire results. It's not unusual to find a "black sheep" in a Sunday birthday family.

NEGATIVE ASPECTS

★

No one really likes to admit to having a nasty side, and most of us do a good job of hiding it. However, it's always good to know what to expect if you catch your partners out on one of their "off" days.

ARIES

As long as Ariens can curl up and keep warm in winter, they're okay; but if they've got to go out in cold, wet weather, they are an insufferable pain in the proverbial. They whine if you're five minutes late and will nag if you're wearing cheap jewelry. Great lecturers on morality, they can make the most of an innocent meeting. Bad losers, when the dog or horse with their money on it struggles in last. All in all, when they're good, they're very very good; *but* when they're bad, they're HORRID.

TAURUS

Bull sometimes can be short for bully, and Taureans can be real pests when they want things done. They see red when people show off, become very sullen when a loan is turned down, and give short shrift to malingerers. They are regular little gluttons, rushing in and taking the last slice of cake or pie. They tend to be the most flatulent of the Zodiac, so steer clear of them when they've had brussels sprouts for dinner. Their code seems to be "after me, you can come first."

GEMINI

Short on patience, Geminis abhor slow drivers and those who think only of themselves. Don't read the paper or magazine before they do, or you'll see a tantrum like you haven't seen before. The eternal Peter Pan of the Zodiac, a Gemini is like an extra child in the household. Geminians rarely shut up from the moment they wake up until they go to bed. The best investment if you're living with this sign is a pair of earplugs. You'll probably also have a garage of unfinished projects.

CANCER

To keep the adult Cancerian happy, you'll have to have a ready supply of food and drink. Cancerians won't wait for you to set the table; they'll just tuck the napkin in and draw up a chair to the fridge. They get upset when the bathroom scales go overboard, and they'll go off the deep end when you throw all their rubbish out. They are the biggest slobs of the Zodiac, and they always leave a ring around the bath. They embroider the truth when it suits them.

LEO

Bossy, arrogant, and chauvinistic are some of the nicer adjectives we can give to Leos. Growls when they have to wear hand-me-downs, sulks if they're relegated to second best, and they hibernate in winter. Without a doubt the vainest of the star signs, and you can be mistaken in thinking they're all brawn and no brain. They love to be center stage and will do a song and dance routine when they open the fridge and the light comes on.

VIRGO

If you want to be a martyr, spend some time with a Virgo; it'll really make you appreciate what you've got. Critical of others, but at times uncommunicative themselves, Virgos belong to one of the hardest signs to understand. They shudder at grubby underwear and balk at dirty nails. The biggest hypochondriacs of all, they are supposed to be "the salt of the earth." Rubbish—Epsom salts is more likely. They race around emptying ashtrays or washing dishes before you've even finished with them.

LIBRA

This is the sign that the adage "street angel, house devil" was coined for, as most long-suffering Libra partners will vouch for. Social climbers prone to nervous breakdowns because of their indecisiveness, Librans can be emotionally draining. Two-timing is part of their makeup, but when *you* do it, watch out. When they've been drinking, they will nag nonstop, but when sober, they're mealy-mouthed and pious.

SCORPIO

There aren't enough nasty words to go round when Scorpios trot out their true colors. Surly, secretive, and sarcastic are traits that are second nature to them, but they can't take it when it's dealt back. They sink into black moods and can go days without being civil. Insanely jealous, this is the sign that is likely to commit crimes of passion. They *never* forget a past indiscretion but expect you to overlook their extracurricular activities.

SAGITTARIUS

Loud-mouthed bores and frank to the point of downright rudeness, it's a wonder these people ever keep a friend. They tend to gamble the housekeeping if they are male, and they'll squirrel it away in a separate bank account if they're female. Lazy and unfeeling, they enjoy being in the limelight. Exhibitionists and egotists, they tend to live beyond their means. Keeping up with the Joneses is very important to this sign.

CAPRICORN

Boring is the negative of Capricorn. Dull, dreary, and restrictive, half an hour's time spent in this person's company will have you climbing the wall. Capricorns can make mountains out of molehills, are holier than thou, and often teetotal; everything about them seems gray. As an Earth sign, they have to take care that if they stand still for too long they'll grow roots, and dogs will mistake them for trees and pee on them. They can also get palpitations just at the thought of spending money.

AQUARIUS

Negative Aquarians are off the planet without smoking pot. Vitriolic, kinky, superficial gossip mongers and busybodies, they work only when they want, and too bad if it puts anyone else out. They tend to be the biggest "know-it-alls" when in fact they know very little. Usually when they put the mouth in motion, they find they have a foot in it. This is the person who makes castles in the air and then goes to live in them. Never believe what Aquarians tell you, as it changes from day to day.

PISCES

Watch out if Pisces show you their negative side, as you could be in for quite a shock. Wishy-washy wet blankets who, under the influence of drugs or drink, can become liars and cheats. They think nothing of taking all the hot water, are often bisexual, lack ambition, and are hopelessly romantic. They look at life through rose-colored glasses, are oversexed and usually the biggest tease of the Zodiac. They lack ambition and are quite happy to freeload.

PETS
AND YOU

★

Have you ever noticed how some dogs look like their owners or vice versa? Particular types of people tend to buy animals that suit their personalities and this often happens with the Zodiac signs. My Virgo dog was chosen for Ken, who's a Scorpio. I particularly wanted a sign that would get on with the whole family and this he does. He also has the fussy eating habits of a Virgo. My other dog is cusp Aries/Taurus and is half the size of the Virgo, but a hundred percent more aggressive. He will chase anything that moves, even if it's four times his size, thanks to his Aries nature. The Taurus side shows through in the form of a very sweet tooth; he can smell chocolates and cake even before they are out of the wrapper.

ARIES

Animals born under the sign of Aries would get on well with Leo, Sagittarius, Gemini, Libra, and Aquarius owners. They tend to be a little insecure at times but on the whole make excellent pets. They also make good show animals, as they enjoy the discipline and organization that this requires. Easily trained, these dogs are invaluable in police and security work. Most Aries people prefer large dogs around them and would be likely to choose Dobermans, Irish setters, or German shepherds. For those living in small houses, corgis would be a good choice. Aries dogs feel the heat and need to be watched closely for heat exhaustion in the summer months.

TAURUS

You'll find a lot of Taureans can take or leave animals, so quiet, well-behaved pets last a lot longer in this household than noisy excitable ones do. Rabbits are often favored, as are cats. Taurean animals respond best to Virgo, Capricorn, Scorpio, Cancer, and Pisces people. They are veritable guzzlers and will eat all the scraps off the plates plus anything else they can get their greedy little jaws around. Consequently, they are often overweight and lazy. They should be desexed at an early age, as they are prolific producers. Keep a close eye on your flowers, as gardening is their favorite sport.

Taureans often choose bull terriers, boxers, or labradors as pets.

GEMINI

Geminis often have more than one animal in the place, not to mention the canary that never shuts up. They prefer small breeds that have indefatigable energy, but often get involved with greyhounds. Gemini owners are often in trouble with the neighbors or tradesmen because their dogs are noisy and have a penchant for legs, bikes, and cars. The duality of Gemini owners is shown to perfection in the sizes and breeds they choose. For example, they'll often have a miniature specimen yapping round your legs as you walk in the front door while at the same time they'll be straining to hold the Great Dane on the leash. Their love of the outdoors and any sporting event manifests itself in the training of whippets and greyhounds. Signs that get on with the Gemini pet are Libra, Aquarius, and Leo, but don't expect the household to be quiet.

CANCER

Cancerian animals are home and family oriented, and it's often the pet born under this sign that travels hundreds of miles to go back to a former home. Woe betide a master or mistress who throws out a favorite rug or toy. They'll be on the receiving end of baleful looks and hangdog expressions for days. These animals enjoy family outings, especially to the beach, and will play with children for hours. Cancerian pets can be a bit moody and may be quite jealous of new pets being brought into the house. Ideally they should be house dogs and shouldn't be left alone for hours on end; otherwise, they are apt to get on the neighbors' nerves with their howling. Compatible signs for a Cancer pet are Pisces and Virgo. A large proportion of Cancerian people feel a little insecure, and for this reason, they prefer large breeds such as English pointers, weimaraner, spaniels, and German shepherds.

LEO

The sign of Leo is easy to pick in animals. Their haughty demeanor and natural arrogance puts them head and shoulders above the rest. These signs love to be the center of attention and react well to applause in the show ring. Never laugh at Leo pets or make them do tricks; it just isn't in their nature to act the clown. Human Leos usually have a great affinity with cats. I suppose this strikes a chord in their nature somewhere, and the home is often graced by Siamese or Burmese breeds. Obviously the most expensive breed is preferred, reflecting the Leo's love of having the best. Because the Lion is a great hunter, dogs that love to chase a quarry are often chosen, like cattle dogs, Irish wolfhounds, or greyhounds. Most Leos don't have much time for birds or fish; as pets they class them as pretty ordinary. Suitable owners for a Leo pet are Aries, Sagittarius, Aquarius, and Libra.

VIRGO

Virgos don't care what animal they have as long as it's quiet, easily cleaned, and doesn't reproduce too rapidly. Virgo animals are fussy eaters and born worriers. Your Virgo dog will watch you with a worried look on his or her face if you are going out because it means it's going to be left alone. Virgo dogs will bark loudly at visitors from the safety of your skirts or from behind the chair and will give in without a fight if challenged for a bone. They can become quite excitable when the offer of a walk is made. Because of the ease with which they can be toilet trained, the Virgo pet is ideal for apartment or condominium dwelling, as they'll take quite readily to the kitty litter. Many Virgos choose fox terriers and dachsunds for companionship. Compatible signs would be Pisces, Cancer, and Taurus.

LIBRA

You never know quite what to expect with a human Libra, and you don't fare any better with an animal born under the same sign. You only have to have a slight change in the weather and the Libran cats go crazy, swinging from curtains, making unexpected leaps and twirls, and getting dizzy from chasing their tails. They have minds of their own and will only come inside when they are good and ready. Libra dogs like to be cuddled and have lots of affection lavished on them. They enjoy being groomed and you won't get a smarter duo than the Libra owner and Libra dog going out for a walk. Breeds that appeal to Libras are often the long-haired variety like Old English sheepdogs, collies, Afghan hounds, and Pekinese. Cats chosen are often Persian. A good rapport is found between Aries and Sagittarius owners for this pet sign.

SCORPIO

Scorpio animals are possessive, jealous, and mean. Because of their amorous natures, it's often wise to desex them at an early stage. This probably won't stop your Scorpio tomcat from caterwauling, however. All Scorpios, whether animal or human, are nocturnal creatures and love to go on the prowl at night. Scorpio animals don't make friends or give their love too readily, and most have a standoffish air about them. Dogs born under this sign need a firm hand and plenty of exercise. Like all Scorpios, they love to uncover things and have a great nose for sniffing things out. They do very well in police and customs work. They are highly intelligent and perform well as guide dogs for the blind. Owners should preferably be Taurus, Cancer, and Pisces to get the best out of them. Scorpios often choose pointers, German shepherds, and bloodhounds.

SAGITTARIUS

Like their human counterparts, Sagittarian animals are happy-go-lucky, adventurous, and friendly. Tall fences are no deterrent to a Sagittarian dog if he wants to go exploring; he'll just find another way out. They'll travel for miles when the mood takes them; and because they love children, it's usually the Sagittarius dog that's taking part in all the fun at the school playground. Ideally, this dog or cat sign should be housed on a farm, as it has an affinity with horses. They can be very boisterous; games should be kept low-key, especially where toddlers are concerned, otherwise they could be knocked over. The Sagittarius dog is everyone's friend, even the postman's, but don't be misled into thinking he'd be a pushover for a burglar. When it comes to protecting property, those teeth will be shown in a snarl, not the usual smile. Dogs bred for the outdoor climate are often chosen by the Sagittarian, like St. Bernards, samoyeds, dalmatians, and borzois. Best owners for Sagittarius pets would be Gemini, Aquarius, and Aries.

CAPRICORN

Capricorn animals are very rarely any trouble and, therefore, are ideal for people living in densely populated areas or in confined spaces. These animals won't get out of their own way, so there's no worry about them being classed as a nuisance. Capricorn dogs love to bury bones and it's nothing to find them behind the sofa cushions or under the rose bushes. They get very set in their ways and punctuality is important when it comes to feeding times. They feel the cold, so it's necessary to keep them warm in winter. Ideal owners would be Cancer, Virgo, and another Capricorn. Suitable breeds would be Scottish terrier, basset hound, and dachsund. Capricorn cats are too lazy to catch mice but are great companions, especially for night owl Capricorns. Because they aren't the most active of the pet signs, Capricorn dogs may have the unfortunate problem of flatulence, so food should be fairly bland. Otherwise, invest in gas masks or room fresheners when you are having dinner guests.

AQUARIUS

Aquarians are classed as the humanitarian sign, so it's not unusual to find they have a menagerie of animals of all shapes and sizes. Cats don't really turn them on; after all, they don't *do* anything except sleep, and that to an Aquarian is a waste of time. They prefer animals with a little more get up and go. However, if a cat needed a home, they would be the first to provide it. The human Aquarian is a salesman's dream whenever he or she is headed in the direction of a pet shop or the A.S.P.C.A. Dogs born under the sign of Aquarius love speed and don't know the word fear. It's these intrepid dogs you see riding pillion on motor bikes or perched atop a flat-bed truck with no visible means of support. Aquarian cats are a fireman's nightmare; they always manage to get caught up the highest tree or in the most inaccessible places. Aquarian animals need active owners like Scorpio, Sagittarius, Gemini, and Aries. Best breeds: mixed.

PISCES

They say every Piscean has a bit of witch or warlock in his or her makeup, so it's obvious a cat takes pride of place in this household. Pisces animals have a highly developed sixth sense, and these are the dogs that frequently make the news for rescuing children from pools or warning owners of impending danger. Pisceans, as a whole, love animals, often preferring their company to humans. Their tastes don't just run to cats and dogs. Most Piscean homes would not be complete without the goldfish, birds, or whatever stray animals that have crossed their path. Many Pisceans have made their careers with the training of dolphins or the feeding of sharks in pools. Suitable owners for a Piscean animal would be Scorpio, Cancer, Taurus, and Capricorn. Small breeds that can be cuddled are best, like silky terriers, poodles, and Pomeranians.

SECRETS AND
SUN SIGNS

★

"Listen, do you want to know a secret?" is the type of phrase usually too hard for the average person to resist. Whether it stays confidential is another matter, and the twelve signs of the Zodiac can be found to be very different in their approach to this.

ARIES

Aries people dislike anything that smacks of hidden intrigue. Very often they are in a job that relies on straight talk or information that comes from others such as police work, prisons, the armed services, or the running of government departments and private companies. Consequently, it becomes second nature to lay things on the line, and this can make them unpopular with others. You're far better keeping any juicy tidbits of family gossip to yourself unless you want the Aries to go in to bat for you; and then you'll have to take the rough with the smooth, as this sign doesn't do things by halves.

TAURUS

Taureans often make great confidential secretaries, and it's like pulling teeth to elicit any information from them. They are good listeners, and you can rest assured it will go no further. The only problem is, the poor old Taurus then walks around with this burden weighing heavily on his or her conscience, worrying how it's all going to work out. Because Taureans hate telling lies, they end up withdrawing, and resentment toward the informer sets in. They'd just as soon you didn't tell them anything. After all, they reason, if I'm meant to know about it, I'll hear about it all in good time when it's all open and above board.

GEMINI

Now we've really got trouble. Dear little Geminis just adore a scandal and their keyword is "Communication." There's never any malice intended in their gossip, just the simple act of repeating what they think could interest you. Anyone can weasel a secret out of a Gemini by clever probing and showing avid interest. Give them their due, there's no one better to plant a red herring or send someone off on a wild goose chase, and they are invaluable if you have them on your side to catch a malicious gossiper. Just take a pinch of salt with everything that comes via a Gemini; chances are it's been added to since it was first told.

CANCER

There's no way to get Cancers to spill the beans unless you tank them up with amber fluid. Tough luck if they're teetotal (but that's as scarce as hen's teeth anyway), but if they aren't averse to bending the elbow, you could get lucky and release the floodgates. Ms. Cancer is a little more circumspect than her male counterpart and will hug a secret to her bosom forever and a day, especially if she's been sworn to secrecy about an unexpected engagement or birth. However, if she doesn't care for the informer, she can give a verbal nip with those claws and then run for cover before all hell breaks loose. On the whole, though, your secret should be safe with her.

LEO

Leos like to maintain a close home and family front, so if there's anything amiss, you won't get to hear a whisper of scandal. Children's misdemeanors are hushed up and family quarrels remain private. On the work scene it is a different kettle of fish, and it's each man or woman for themselves. If this means a confidence may have to be broken to jump ahead of the opposition, then Leos have no qualms in doing it. Their love of people makes them suspect regarding secrets because they really are without guile and will spill the beans before they can stop themselves—but only because they like everyone to be part of what's going on.

VIRGO

This sign is often classed as the uncommunicative sign; marvelous if you want a secret kept, but very frustrating if you are trying to prize information out of one of them. Being Mercury-ruled like Gemini, they do have a tendency to expound if someone puts the pressure on or when they feel that it's their moral duty to speak up. The acid tongue of this sign can cut people to shreds, and if the informer is spreading malicious lies or gossip and this comes to the notice of a Virgo, he'll deal with them in no uncertain terms. Unless you are a masochist, just to be on the safe side, find someone else to tell your secret to.

LIBRA

Good old Libra, sitting on the fence, giving and taking no quarter. Forget this sign if you are looking for a great reaction to a succulent morsel of gossip you've picked up, because Librans will see nothing suspicious in the goings-on of others. Totally diplomatic, their motto is "live and let live," and they couldn't give a hoot what's going on next door or down the street. It's very important for Librans to be perfectly balanced, and they wouldn't be able to achieve harmony within themselves if they were worried or concerned about others' private dealings. I wouldn't be surprised to hear that the three wise monkeys had been modeled on Libra.

SCORPIO

Here we have the original secretive sign. Not only will Scorpios keep your secrets but their own as well. Don't ask where they've been or who with; you'll be met by an impenetrable wall of silence. It's the young Scorpios who have the secret societies, teenage Scorpios who have the private diaries, and adult Scorpios who can lead two lives quite happily. I believe Mata Hari was a Scorpio. They make excellent Secret Service agents as well as top detectives because they are great at getting information out of others. When it comes to them divulging confidences, their lips are sealed. Just remember if you've ever blown the cover on a Scorpio, they will pay you back in full, as revenge is very sweet to them.

SAGITTARIUS

What you see is what you get with this open, friendly sign. Try as they might to mind their own business, Sagittarians are like big friendly dogs who come sniffing round for any morsels that come their way. Their natural inquisitiveness loves to keep them up-to-date with current happenings, but their sense of fair play never lets the situation get out of hand. If they feel someone is getting a raw deal, and particularly if that person isn't there to defend himself, Sagittarians will really let the informer have it with both barrels. Once they've heard something, they dismiss it, as they feel life is too short to be cluttered up with problems—and they've usually got enough of their own.

CAPRICORN

Reserve is a natural trait of this sign, so if asked to keep a secret, Capricorns will. However, because of a strong moral code and set business ethics, they may make provisos. Quite definitely, if it's a smutty piece of gossip, they will tell you in no uncertain terms that they're not interested and at the same time you could get a lecture on self-discipline. They make excellent secretaries, priests, and chaplains, as well as counselors, as everyone's right to privacy is very strong in their beliefs. Don't expect Capricorns to be a fund of information on any subject; they go by one of two rules: "Silence is golden" and "Least said is soonest mended."

AQUARIUS

Luckily for us ordinary mortals, Aquarians very rarely come down to earth and when they do, it's like trying to catch quicksilver. If they are told a secret, it usually goes in one ear and out the other, and they usually can't be bothered with the drama that accompanies it. Aquarians rarely give their word to anyone, as this could tie them down; so they make excuses about having to get away when it looks as if a hen party or pub gossip could be on the agenda. They are the most humanitarian of all the signs and certainly won't stand in judgment if by chance something does come to their notice. Their usual reaction is a murmured "Really?" and that's about the extent of it.

PISCES

Another one who loves a secret, either real or one that Pisces have conjured up in their fertile imagination. What little Pisces hasn't had an imaginary friend who has remained secret to everyone but him or herself? One has to be a little careful with this imaginative sign because things can tend to get out of hand. Who do you think started the story about the fish that got away? As with other Water signs, things that go on beneath the surface fascinate them, so secrets, especially if they have romantic overtones, are right up their alley. They'd love someone to confide in them about a midnight elopement or a lover. If it were me, I'd tell Pisces just so much and no more and let them have the enjoyment of embroidering it.

SPORTING SIGNS

ARIES

This person is a fighter thanks to the ruling planet Mars, the war god. Obviously Ariens do well in boxing, but they attack any sport with the same dedication and will to win. They enjoy team effort. They also enjoy wrestling and car racing. Aries women are very vocal when on the sidelines and make terrific coaches for school basketball teams.

TAURUS

Nothing too strenuous for this little Bull. Croquet, lawn bowls, a game of badminton, and possibly bowling are fine. Because they tend to carry a bit of excess weight, Taureans don't like too strenuous sports. Ms. Taurus will pack great picnic baskets for those participating and will give constant reassurance to competitors as long as she isn't asked to compete actively.

GEMINI

The more dangerous sports appeal to this sign. Parachuting, hang gliding, and roller skating will draw Geminis like a pin to a magnet, but they also enjoy hot air ballooning, gymnastics, high diving, volleyball, and football. Parents who have Gemini children often spend the best part of the weekend running their children from one sport to another, as Geminis always have more than one project on the go at once.

CANCER

This sign is at home in the water, and Cancers usually do well in any sport on land or sea; swimming, water polo, canoeing, running, squash, table tennis, and trampolining. In fact, people born under this sign can turn their hands to almost any sport and not only succeed but also win trophies. There are usually more sports teachers and coaches born under the sign of Cancer than any other sign of the Zodiac.

LEO

Leos hate to come second and therefore usually do well in any sport they take up. In England they would definitely take part in fox hunts, as they love the thrill of the chase. Game fishing, cycling, weight lifting, and soccer suit them. They love the limelight, so do well as captains of their teams. They hate ridicule and their pride suffers when it takes a beating.

VIRGO

Virgos like to take calculated risks, so sports such as darts, trail bike riding, racewalking, baseball, and softball appeal to them. Any pair sports produce good results with this sign, as there's always a good line of communication between Virgos and their partners. It's a pity this doesn't always follow in a personal relationship.

LIBRA

Balance is part and parcel of this sign's makeup, so Librans make excellent jockeys. They also do well in rowing, gymnastics—particularly the parallel bars—high jump and long jump, golf and shot put. Many Librans leave competitive sports to become great TV or radio commentators. As Air signs, they love to hear the roar of a big crowd egging them on.

SCORPIO

This sign is a formidable enemy, so Scorpios are much better to have on your side. They have excellent eye sight and do well in shooting, darts, bowling, football, swimming, surfing, and archery. They give one hundred percent to their sport and don't mince words if their teammates don't.

SAGITTARIUS

Anything to do with animals, particularly horses, interests a Sagittarius. They like polo, equestrian events, and harness racing. In these sporting events the animals do most of the work, but Sagittarians are talented athletes. Ruled by the muscles of the body, they have to take care they don't injure these areas if they are playing sports professionally. They excel in hurdling, discus throwing, and Ironman triathlon events.

CAPRICORN

What better sport could the sign of the Goat choose than mountaineering? This is a very surefooted sign and Capricorns do particularly well in soccer, ice skating, cross-country running, skiing, tennis, ballet, ballroom dancing, and fencing. As this sign is more academically inclined than sports-minded, it's not surprising to find them treasurers of the sports club instead of part of the team. They also do well in martial arts or judo.

AQUARIUS

This is the sign that lives in the fast lane; so obviously the more exciting the sport, the better it is. Flying, barefoot waterskiing, shooting the rapids, windsurfing, drag racing, and competition table tennis are their sports, to name a few. The only problem with this sign is that Aquarians tend to be know-it-alls, as their dominant theme is "I know," and as coaches they never stop nagging.

PISCES

As with the other two Water signs, Cancer and Scorpio, Pisces is totally at home in or on the water. Yachting, or any other type of sailing, scuba diving, water ballet, and any of the winter snow sports usually produce trophies from an early age. They are slippery little customers and often do well as kickers in a football team or goalies in hockey. They lack ambition, so if they're serious about their sport, they will have to be pushed.

SEX AND YOUR
STAR SIGN

★

ARIES

Ariens love leather. Not that they're into anything
kinky, but let someone meander by when an Aries
is out on the prowl and they happen to be in a
leather miniskirt, leather boots, or leather pants,
and that's it, just a matter of time until that Aries
fire turns into a volcano. When you turn this little
lamb into a raging Ram, make sure you know
what you're doing. Ariens get uptight at "teasers"
and frown upon promiscuity. If you can't afford
the leather enticements, the next best thing is
lambswool. A soft rug, bedspread, or even car
seat covers will have them pawing the ground in
anticipation.

The female is by far the more liberated of this

sign. She enjoys lovemaking and will often pick a fight before bedtime so she can kiss and make up. She keeps her flame on low simmer, ready to have it stoked when the time is right. She's a very private person and won't discuss her bedroom antics, even with her closest friend. Mind you, she's quite interested in learning what others get up to so she can add it to her repertoire. She is the aggressor in a relationship that has a quieter sign as a partner, which of course delights him.

The male Arien worries. Was his performance satisfactory? Did he satisfy her? Could he improve on his technique? Will he compare favorably to her last guy? As a result, before he gets up nerve to repeat the performance, he has to have a quick drink to boost his confidence. Too many of these liquid injections then mar the performance he's trying so hard to better. If he asked the lady straight out how it was, she would assure him it was terrific and he'd save wear and tear on many organs. He's not averse to a little fantasy, so to whet his appetite, greet him in a French maid's outfit or play doctors and nurses because he loves uniforms.

TAURUS

Buy some satin sheets and you're in like Flynn with this sign. Once you master the art of catching Taureans as they shoot out of the bed like missiles, you can have some loving, intimate moments. Don't pounce on them, they don't like commando-like raids on their soft lights, sweet music, and subtle perfume or after-shave. They are an "earthy" sign, so a walk in the woods could see many a Bull being led by the horns. Don't skimp on that special dinner date if you're hoping to get a reward at the end of the evening. Taureans hate cheapskates.

Mr. Bull is about as subtle as a steamroller when it gets down to the nitty-gritty. He tends to be a "wham, bam, thank you ma'am" lover, but he is willing to be educated and makes a very industrious student. He is pretty shortsighted, so he'll fumble and stumble around in the dark until he's learned where you are, but he's considerate and romantic in his own way. He'll bellow with appreciation if you parade in your birthday suit and his appetite, like that of all bulls, is prodigious. A sexy red nightie would also be like the proverbial red rag to a Bull.

Ms. Bull is as basic as you can get. If she wants you, she'll take you, and who'd be silly enough to refuse the charms of this little bovine? She is usually well-endowed and lovemaking is a very natural function for her. It feeds a deep primordial urge, and as the most procreative sign, she gets pregnant quicker than anyone else, so be careful. She's always starving after her bouts in the bed, and she'll bring back a feast to eat there and then. She has a nose like a bloodhound and will be turned on by the smell of after-shave or masculine soap. She'll also be turned off just as quickly by dirty nails and body odor.

GEMINI

If you want to go for seconds, then you'd better bed a Gemini. This dual sign can move from idling into top gear without the slightest trouble, and many a lady has found herself being compromised before she knew it. This Air sign is an honorary member of "the mile high club" and sometimes doesn't even have to leave the ground. Communication is the keyword here, so if you want a Gemini's body, ask for it. Playing mind games turns this sign off quicker than anything. You could be told where to get off when you ask, but at least there's communication. Geminis tend to say one thing and do another, so you'd better find out where home base is before you hit a home run.

He is a bag of hot air at times and loves to give orders. Learn to lip-read if you're embarking on a relationship and invest in a pair of earmuffs. Very charming when he's out and about socializing, but at times he fails to practice what he preaches. Geminis lose interest quickly, so don't keep him dangling or put him on a promise. If you do, he may not be around when you are ready, willing, and able. Exciting sports such as car racing, skiing, or hang gliding will make him romantic and set him out on his own quest for adventure.

She is in two minds the whole time she's being

courted, probably because she has to make a decision about one of the fellows. Her mind is racing full-time, and she's often less than popular when she muses out loud, "I mustn't forget to defrost the meat" or "I'll have to repaint that corner of the ceiling" just at the most crucial point of the lovemaking. If she has a beef about her guy's technique, she'll tell him, and then wonder why he takes offense. She's always planning some little rendezvous to add a little spice to the relationship, and she's never boring.

CANCER

This sign is a "would be if could be, but mostly they don't" type of person. Cancers are in love with love and often play out a love scene they've seen at the movies. Rhett Butler and Scarlett O'Hara move over, there's someone else acting out your role. Sentimentalists, they need a lot of understanding, and if the notion takes them to make love in the rain or on a secluded beach, then go along with them. They are tender, gentle lovers—no good for those who like a more forceful type of partner.

A crab never finds getting from point A to point B a simple task because of all the sidetracking that goes on. Mr. Cancer can have many dalliances in his life, all without meaning to, and still maintain he's happily married. Pierce his shell and you find you've got yourself a marshmallow, soft, sweet, and clinging. A water bed will be a source of never-ending pleasure, and he's one that will corner you in the shower, invite you into the bath to play with his toy submarine, or lure you into the Jacuzzi with a bottle of champagne.

Cancer women are ruled by the breasts and stomach, so the idea here is to feed her and then caress her. There's no point in being impatient if you're wooing her; she likes to spend plenty of time in the bathroom preparing for seduction. Buy her a single red rose and she'll swoon with delight; tell her that you love her constantly. Ask her to cut her nails if you're having an illicit relationship, as she tends to use those pincers on your back, leaving telltale marks. She doesn't like "quickies" and gets emotionally involved in every liaison.

LEO

Loving Leos can be like living alongside a volcano: you never know when they are about to erupt, and when they do, someone is going to get burned. This sign is a Fire sign and Leos attract others like a flame does a moth. They are also ruled by the heart and, unfortunately, have a few emotional battle scars to prove it. They are an extremely jealous sign and egotists to boot, so when their pride takes a fall, they don't do it by halves. A prospective lover will notice they curl up in front of an open fire on a bearskin rug, purring before the action even begins.

The male Leo does a lot of roaring, but can be as gentle as a kitten in the right hands. He feels very important in the bedroom and needs to be told he's the greatest lover, the handsomest man in creation, and the envy of all the other males. He'll not only believe it but expect it. Scratch him on the tummy and behind the ears and he won't bother to go out tomcatting. He'd love mirrors in the headboard of the bed so he can applaud his own performance. Tell him he's just so-so as a lover and he'll sulk for days.

The Lioness is used to stalking in the jungle and enjoys the thrill of the chase. Not for her the guy who plays straight into her hands, but one she can round up and pounce on when she's ready. She'll nip, scratch, and bite in lovemaking and isn't worried if she has to set the pace. Very conscious of her good body, she'll parade around in the altogether until she's sure her lover has fully appreciated what he's about to receive. She won't tolerate playing second fiddle and demands constant homage. This lady when she gets going will almost set the covers alight, so wear fireproof gear.

VIRGO

Virgo is such a complex sign that it's difficult to imagine Virgos getting excited without analyzing and criticizing their reasons for it. For example, imagine a Virgo eyeing someone at a disco: "Hmm, she looks nice, but I wonder why she wears her hair like that" or "I don't like his taste in clothes." Virgos just can't help themselves. They don't know how to switch off and just relax for the sake of relaxing without having to account for their reasons. They rarely have more than two children once they're married. The first one usually arrives as a bit of a fluke, the second, just to see how that fluke occurred.

The male Virgo has lots of naughty thoughts but doesn't know how to make them real. He will go over his plan of action again and again in his mind until it's letter perfect, but when it comes to putting his thoughts into action, there's a communication breakdown. He's not terribly romantic— about as exciting as a bowl of porridge and as quiet as a mouse when he finally gets under way. What you see is what you get, no frills but a deep and meaningful relationship. Given a few lessons in the art of making love, he will blossom like a late rosebud. His sign, "I think," will have him thinking up some new variations on an old theme that will be worth waiting for.

Ms. Virgo likes to fuss. She'll run around with the air freshener to remove cigarette smells, rinse her mouth with Listerine to combat bad breath, and rarely will she let herself go in bed enough to wrinkle the bed linen. Cleanliness is next to godliness and romance runs a poor third. Her sign is "the Virgin" and she remains that, mentally, if not physically. A quick tumble is not her scene, and she is often turned on by an intellectual person rather than a he-man type. When she does give her body and soul, she does it with the thoroughness expected of this sign. She won't shortchange you in the bedroom, but she doesn't linger at the scene too long afterwards either.

LIBRA

Taureans could learn a few tricks of the trade from their cosign, Libra. This loving, sensuous sign is happiest on cloud nine and doesn't make any apologies for it. Librans may turn up late for a rendezvous, but they make up for it; they love almost as if there's no tomorrow. They cut their teeth on the Kama Sutra, and the bedroom is the best designed and equipped room in the house. They have been known to swing, but as they are a dual sign, who can blame them? When courting Librans, be decisive. They have enough hassles trying to make up their own minds about things. They hate fights, so don't pick on them just before bedtime.

The male Libra is Mr. Casanova, Rudolph Valentino, and Adam all rolled into one. He oozes charm, has a sexy way of walking, and a line straight out of sexy romance novels. The trouble is, you can't believe any of it. He's the type you should stay engaged to, at least for thirty years, because he does a Dr. Jekyll and Mr. Hyde turnabout once he gets to the altar. A charming companion, witty conversationalist with an insatiable libido, this fellow will expect you to be as supple as a gymnast and as adventurous as any explorer in the bed. He'll swing from the chandeliers by one foot while his hands and mouth are going nonstop. The mouth is talking, I hasten to add. He'll forget you as soon as he's had you.

Ms. Libra isn't as superficial as her male cosign. Her body language comes through loud and clear, but there's nothing crass about it. She enjoys being loved, doesn't care if it's not a long-term commitment as long as the guy is sincere in his attentions while they are together. She usually has a great body and is particularly well-endowed breast-wise. Of course she dresses to show off this good cleavage. Sexy lingerie like garter belts and stockings, slinky panties, and a good sexy movie or book will put her in the mood for love. This lady will stay wrapped in her lover's arms all night, as she enjoys his body so much.

SCORPIO

Lucky you if you've managed to snare this half-wild creature. Scorpios will run like startled gazelles if they don't fancy you, but if the chemistry is right, you're in for a right royal treat, a veritable smorgasbord of tasty tidbits to enhance your nightlife. This is an all or nothing sign, so don't cry wolf if you don't want to be eaten. Realize that a session in bed with this lusty person will test your sexual prowess and stamina to the hilt. Scorpios often find their reputations precede them, and the opposite sex shivers in anticipation when they are introduced. Total honesty in a relationship coupled with trust are the criteria here.

His magnetism hits you like a laser beam and you've been zapped into another dimension. He comes straight to the point and tells you "I want your body," but says it in such a way you can't take offense. Memorize his name, as he has no sense of humor if you call him by your ex's name by mistake. He walks softly but carries a big stick, and it's like venturing into a minefield when you take on this liaison. Life is a game of chess and you are his pawn. He won't tell you he loves you that often because the very fact he's there should be enough. Make sure there's an element of surprise in your lovemaking, and never make the mistake of putting sex on a roster basis or you'll be a partner short.

She is dubbed a "femme fatale" rather unfairly. The minute she tells her date she's a Scorpio, his eyes light up and he starts drooling at what has dropped into his hands. He's probably out of luck as Scorpio women aren't into one-night stands and prefer their fellows to do the chasing. A good bottle of red wine may loosen a Scorpio's inhibitions, but be warned, fellows, she is a witch at heart and can put a spell on you in no time flat. Once into a relationship she will sap a man's energy so totally he'll need to head for a health spa to recuperate.

SAGITTARIUS

This sign is half horse, half man, and when necessary, Sagittarians certainly gallop off into the sunset with *your* heart and without any commitment. The grass is always greener on the other side of the fence, so of course they're going to be tempted to graze; but unless someone lets the barriers down, they won't do any great harm. Happy-go-lucky, friendly, cheerful people, they tend to get under your skin before you know it, but they take off the minute the other party gets soppy or serious. Beware of Sagittarians met on vacations. Their theme is "travel," and they'll enter into the spirit of a shipboard romance or other meetings, but that's all it is, just a fling.

Mr. Sagittarius loves offbeat furnishings like mirrors on the ceilings, oddly shaped bedside lamps, or beds that massage your back. He professes to be very macho, hanging out in male-dominated domains, but he's not much at delivering the goods. Perhaps there are a few deep-seated skeletons in the closet that may need looking at. Not all Sagittarian males are like this. There are the odd one or two that perform very well and, as a Fire sign, a Sagittarian should be a red hot lover, sweeping his partner along on a wave of passion. He will, however, be out pumping iron at the gym instead of . . . the obvious.

Thank goodness one of the Sagittarians is good in bed. Ms. S. is frank, has a good appetite, and really enjoys her indoor sports. It's not unusual to find a collection of balls in her bedroom. She's a keen tennis and basketball player. If someone puts the hard word on her or makes a pass at her, she'll deftly block it, or counterattack, depending on the mood she's in. She gets turned on by big men and shows of strength. She'd be interested in a picnic if you're planning to take her down the garden path, as the outdoors appeals.

CAPRICORN

Forget any ambitious plans you might be thinking of trying out with this sign because Capricorns just won't be in it. Sex is a very private pastime as far as they're concerned and, as they go through life wearing blinkers, ear plugs, and mouth guards, they're not likely to learn anything new. This is not to say they don't enjoy their love life—far from it—as long as it's at night, with the blinds down, the lights off, and the neck-to-knee night-wear in place, everything will go as expected. There's rarely a change in routine either, as this sign is a creature of habit. Variety is definitely not the spice of life with this sign.

Mr. Goat can leap from bed to bed as well as the rest of the single guys, but once he settles down into a permanent relationship, his leap becomes a sedate hop. He is quite highly sexed, but he hasn't really learned to play his partner like a harp; in fact, his fiddle needs tuning. He is a man of few words and even fewer actions and seems to be programmed for expediency. He is a good pupil, however, and a patient partner can do wonders with him. Think of him as a lump of clay you're going to mold and you'll end up with an objet d'art. Keep him moving; otherwise, like all Earth signs, he could get into a rut and become deadly boring.

She's fine until the bills come in and this will preoccupy her when she's making love. She's a little shy, so don't come on too strong until she gives you the come-on. This may be so laid-back, you could even miss it. A very deep sign, you may have to court her for weeks before you get anywhere near first base. She's very fussy, so she'll do a mental stock-take on the first date to see if you pass muster. Allow her to get changed in the bathroom, as she doesn't go in for birthday suits. She is faithful, loving, and loyal but lacks a spirit of adventure. Don't talk dirty to her or she'll freeze up; instead, stroke her gently and tell her you love her and you won't get a sweeter lover.

AQUARIUS

Do you want a flight of fancy? Are you interested in soaring to great heights? Are you bored with routine? If the answer is yes to these three questions, nab yourself an Aquarian. Aquarian's nutty approach is a certain cure for boredom. This is the sign that will make love there and then. As long as there's a lock on the door and blinds that shut, they can enact their own close encounter. They never put off till tomorrow what can be done today, as that's one they'll never get again. Forbidden fruits excite them, so they live dangerously, setting up secret trysts with other people's partners just for the hell of it. Some Aquarians, on the other hand, are confirmed bachelors and spinsters and live exemplary lives.

You need your skates on if you're going to catch the male. He moves like greased lightning and usually has hordes of women hanging off his arms. He is gentle and kind and tells his women exactly what they want to hear. The only one who doesn't believe it is him. He writes great scripts and acts them out to the letter. At times you can talk to him and get no reaction. The light's on, but there's no one home. He needs his own space and won't thank you for violating it. He can be cold, as the higher you fly, the colder and more rarified the atmosphere gets. You can't cage this bird, so just enjoy him and then let him free.

This little lady is a free spirit. She gives no quarter and expects none in return. Don't give her ultimatums or she'll thumb her nose at you. Be tolerant, antinuclear, nonracist, and a champion of lost causes, and you'll be talking her language. Dress in bright plumage because this little bird likes her guy to strut like a peacock. When she finds the time to mate, she is straightforward, basic, and generous. Take note, however; her quirky sense of humor can surface at any given time, so a partner mustn't take her too seriously. Leave the door of the love nest open at all times, and your little pigeon will come home to roost.

PISCES

You can never be sure with Pisces if they are genuine or just darn good actors or actresses. If it's the latter, they certainly deserve an Oscar for best supporting role. They are dreamy, sensitive people who like to get as far away as possible from the day's cares once night falls, and they'll build a wild night around the bedroom. It's in this closet you'll uncover many skeletons, but what goes on in the privacy of the boudoir is a matter that concerns only the participants. They like to playact and adore see-through negligees, champagne to provide rose-colored glasses, and a lover who will have them swimming in the Sea of Tranquillity.

Although this fellow comes under the sign of "the fish," he can be a shark, slowly circling his prey. He's a slippery little customer, also, and no amount of baiting the hook will catch him if he's not interested. He does everything to excess and sex will be tried in the bath, the pool, anywhere where there is water. Watch out for this one on cruises; he doesn't surface the whole time. He is also a master at the art of two-timing; don't believe anything he says. Also be wary if he brings flowers or chocolates; he's definitely got a guilty conscience. The best way to deal with him is to give him a dose of his own medicine now and again.

Ms. Pisces comes beautifully packaged but can be as lethal as a piranha or barracuda. She'll eat you up and spit you out before you've had time to say "thanks." She practices the art of seduction so well you'd think she had lessons from Mata Hari or Cleopatra, and she doesn't walk, she wiggles and glides like a mermaid. She likes to be rewarded with a hug or a kiss now and again, and if she doesn't feel like making love, she'd like just to cuddle up without her partner getting all randy. She'll be a bit moody at times, but it's nothing personal; and when she's shaken the blues off, she'll be ready to partake in whatever little play you may be ready to perform in.

WHAT MAKES THE OTHER SIGN TICK?

ARIES

How do you know if an Aries is interested in you? Certainly Ariens are not the type to come straight out with it, and this can be very frustrating for those on the receiving end of the romance. This sign loves to be needed, so first and foremost you have to appeal to their protective nature. Refined flirting is okay, but anything more is out. So, girls, put away the heavy makeup and the see-through dress, and guys, you can forget that "come up and see my etchings" routine. Being a Fire sign, Aries warm to people who are bright and happy and therefore can be found in abundance at barbecues, car races, and old school reunions.

Ariens often take jobs in government organizations; so for unattached Leos, Sagittarians, Libras, Geminis, and Aquarians, it may be time to have a change of job if your present romance is going downhill. While we're on the subject of love, if you're an Aries and feel romance is passing you by, it could be that you've gotten yourself tangled up with an Earth sign. Nothing irks Aries more than being told what to do. This only makes them more determined not to do it.

Security is very important to this sign, so don't ask to be taken to the most expensive restaurant or expect them to paint the town red with you. They'd much rather save their hard-earned money and buy something they can see is worthwhile and go out to somewhere a little less expensive. That way they can have the best of two worlds. Restraint is the keyword when you set your cap at an Aries. Restraint in dress, manner, speech, and action. Follow this rule and you'll be rewarded with faithfulness and trust.

TAURUS

Now it's no good being sneaky about your intentions if you've got a Taurus in your sights. This sign doesn't understand mind games. What you see is what you get with this little Bull. If you wish to go out with one, then state your intentions loudly and clearly. Silks and satins please a Taurus, so when you dress, make sure that you wear a shirt or blouse of this material.

This sign is basically shy, so although Taureans may appear to be the life and soul of the party, it's not always the case. So don't make the mistake of showing them up in public or you'll never see them again. Taureans get on very well with the other Earth signs, Virgo and Capricorn; and the Water signs, Cancer, Scorpio, and Pisces, have very little trouble with the chemistry. However, if you are a Sagittarius or Aquarius, you may find you don't see eye to eye.

Taureans adore food, and the way to their heart is definitely through their stomach; and because they are often called the banking sign, they would much rather eat at home than spend money on restaurants. Soft lights, sweet music, subtle aromas of perfume or after-shave mixing with delicious dinner smells, and you've got this little Bull contentedly chewing the cud. A word of warning though; don't be taken in by his apparent easygoing nature. Taureans won't and can't be bulldozed into saying or doing anything that they aren't ready to do. Oh! and before I forget, plan at least six months in advance if you have designs on this sign. They hate sudden change, so gently brainwash them to your way of thinking.

GEMINI

The song says "June is bustin' out all over," and for those born in June, this applies as well. There they are, all buzzing around like bees in a bottle, not one of them stopping long enough for anyone to catch them; very disheartening for a Libra, Aquarius, Leo, Aries, or Sagittarius who would love to get to know them a little better. It's not really that difficult, as these aforementioned signs can get to first base very easily with a Gemini.

The Fire signs will attract a Gemini like the proverbial moth to a flame, while the Air signs are already on the same wavelength. Pisces and Capricorn could have their work cut out, though, if they set out to catch this little butterfly. Communication is the keyword here. It's no good sitting in a corner pining for members of this sign. Go out and mix with the crowd that surrounds them. Take up roller or ice skating, hang gliding; or just toddle off to the local disco where they will be found in abundance.

No-nos for those trying to get on the right side of Geminis are sulks, jealousy, and possessive behavior. You can kiss your love good-bye if you do any of these things. They're not terribly practical, so once a relationship is formed, it's the other person who has to balance the budget. Mercury-ruled, this sign can change as easily as the mercury dropping in a barometer, so never make the mistake of taking them for granted, and woe betide if you are silly enough to take them on in an argument. They adore impractical actions, and an unexpected present, a hug, or kiss will mean more than any practical approach.

CANCER

Trying to pin a Cancerian down is about as easy as catching a fish without a line. This sensitive sign retreats as soon as the going gets rough and, once hurt, won't repeat the process. To woo this sign one must have patience, understanding, and a love of home and family. With the warmer weather coming, the best place to meet a Cancerian is at a pool party or on the beach.

Cancerians are rarely the life and soul of the party, preferring to sit on the sidelines and take it all in. If you want to get on with this sign, you must be nice to their dog or cat; as a matter of fact, a good way to meet this sign is to take your own pet for a walk in the park. Don't come on too strong; Cancerians prefer to feel their way around a relationship before they commit themselves. Ruled by the Moon, they can be very emotional and lady Crabs can cry at the drop of a hat, so don't be too rough on her, fellows.

The Earth and Water signs are most compatible with this sign, and know instinctively that the way to get under that hard shell is to turn up on a date with a bottle of wine or a single red rose. The Air and Fire signs find Cancers too deep and lose interest fairly quickly, but not before the poor little Crab has had his or her fingers burned. This sign has a motto, "Love me, love my family," so any of you who balk at the idea of meeting Mom and Dad may as well not bother going on. There's no way a Cancerian will make a move unless he or she has the backing of the family. Besides, prospective suitors have to learn to cook like Mom before they pass muster.

LEO

Spring is the traditional time for blossoming and our little Leo is found flexing his or her muscles in no uncertain terms. After the long cold winter months, Leos start purring as the warm sun offers lazy days and languid nights. To catch Leos off guard, one has to be very smart; they aren't the king and queen of the jungle for nothing. Flattery is their Achilles' heel and this works far better than any head-on attack. Male Leos will puff up with importance if you delegate responsibility to them, and as long as you don't cast aspersions on their masculinity, they will strut like a peacock showing off his plumage.

Lady Leos adore the bright lights and people who are extroverted and fun loving. Obviously, you won't go to a symphony concert or a library if you have your sights set on this sign. Points to remember when going out with a Leo are: wear bright colors; learn to dance; make a mental list of the best restaurants or "in" places to be seen; and keep a steady flow of complimentary remarks directed at them. Gemini, Libra, and Aquarius will do this automatically, whereas Aries and Sagittarius, although very compatible, may find this relationship a mutual admiration society. Scorpio and Capricorn tend to raise the hackles on any self-respecting Lion and often part by mutual consent.

The quickest way to lose the friendship of a Leo is to be disloyal, disagreeable, dishonest, and dismal. A word of warning for all you guys who have been swooning over that lovely Leo Lady: don't make the mistake of going out on a shoe-string budget, or you'll never get a second date. Gold is Leo's color and gold diggers they may be, even though they probably don't realize it.

VIRGO

If you had a few thousand light-years up your sleeve, you'd still be behind the eight ball trying to work out a Virgo. Nonetheless, because it's spring, many feel inspired enough to try and find what makes this sign tick. Rule number one, fellows, is never ask a Virgo woman out while you are unshaven or have the grease from the car still under your fingernails. She'll look at you as though you've just crawled out from under a rock, no matter how good your intentions are. Secondly, she is a stickler for punctuality, so allow some leeway for parking, etc. before stipulating a time.

Mr. Virgo is often uncommunicative, posing a problem for the lady who is trying to capture his interest. Appearing helpless is usually a good tactic, or bringing up the subject of health foods and exercise, as most male Virgos take an interest in keeping their bodies fit.

If you wish to end a relationship with Virgo (Sagittarius and Libra take note), you embarrass them in public, poke fun at their exercises, practice being a slob, or knock their cooking. On the other hand, if you want to attract them, enter into lively debates, express interest in the best show in town, say you like cats and hate clutter, and be lavish in your praise when they show you their pet project.

When dressing to please a Virgo, tone everything down a scale, make sure it is spotless and the color subdued. Women, remember, no chipped nail polish, stockings without runs, and seams, if any, to be dead straight. Guys, this little lady is old-fashioned and adores having car doors opened, chairs pulled out, and the man to walk on the outside of her. In return you'll get an attentive, attractive, well-mannered partner who can be taken home to meet the family without any trauma.

LIBRA

This is probably the greatest charmer of all the signs. Venus-ruled, Librans believe love makes the world go round and fall in and out of love very easily. More often than not, it's the one on the receiving end of the Libra charm that gets hurt because, typically of an Air sign, a Libra promises a lot, but doesn't deliver the goods.

It's not easy to keep up with the swinging moods of this sign, so the best thing to do is steer a middle course. Never be caught gossiping; injustice is a cardinal sin in any Libran's book of morals, and it's dirty pool to knock someone who isn't there to retaliate. Another no-no is snobbery; to a Libra every person is equal, regardless of race or creed. Libras don't like to be rushed; they have to weigh the pros and cons, so ask for a date at least a week before, and if it's a female Libra, don't make advance bookings to wrestling or boxing matches; chances are she may prefer the ballet or the opera.

Libras enjoy outdoor pursuits and keeping in touch with nature—ice skating, hang gliding, parachuting, or sailing are all activities you may have to familiarize yourself with. Ms. Libra enjoys being coy, so don't expect to know where you stand for quite a while, fellows. Mr. Libra will lead the girls a merry dance. He will be very much in demand, as his bright wit and charming personality make him very popular.

If you are a jealous Scorpio or clinging Cancer, you could end up getting hurt. Aquarius can keep this sign evenly balanced as can Aries and Leo. Colors that attract a Libra are blue for the sky, silver for the lightning speed at which they move, and gray because of the indecision that clouds their thinking at times. Harmony is all-important, so don't turn up on a date wearing polka dots and stripes.

SCORPIO

Most of the books depict Scorpios as the "sexy" sign. Granted they are very attractive to the opposite sex, but promiscuous, never. Many a fellow has been set back in his tracks by the icy glare that meets his approach when he comes on too strong. To make your match with a Scorpio, you need to understand the workings of this intricate mind. For instance, Mr. Scorpio is a fighter and therefore loves a challenge. While ever the thrill of the chase is there, he will be among the front-runners, but as soon as his quarry is snared, he will lose interest. The moral of this story, girls, is keep him guessing. Never lose the mystery that surrounds you, that's what fascinates him. He prefers women who have a little gray matter up top. Vacuous people leave him cold, so forget about playing the dumb blonde.

The Air signs, Libra, Gemini, and Aquarius, find this sign very difficult, mainly because Scorpios will not be drawn into arguments and often retreat into sullen silence—very unsettling for an Air sign. Fire signs often fail with this simmering volcano because of their love of organizing. This is one sign that is its own boss, both male and female.

For the fellows who are smitten by this magnetic sign, here's a fairly foolproof rule of thumb— look at her when she's talking to you so she can give you the full impact of those arresting eyes; it also helps to mesmerize you. Talk to her about your work; most Scorpio women hold down very responsible jobs and respect others who are doing likewise. Take her to the scariest movie in town; she's quite at home in the dark—besides, it gives you more of an excuse to put your arm round her. And last, but not least, whether it's Mr. or Ms. Scorpio, DON'T FLIRT!!!! Otherwise you'll be courting disaster.

SAGITTARIUS

The best way to meet a Sagittarian is to plan a trip. This sign is known as the "traveling" sign, so as soon as Sagittarians are old enough to cut the apron strings, they are off to greener pastures. Sagittarius is a warm, loving, happy-go-lucky sign and one could be forgiven for believing what they said on a plane, train, bus, ship, or even a bicycle built for two, because at that time they probably meant it. As soon as they land on terra firma, however, it's a different story. They discard all the trappings from the last trip and prepare to set off on a new one.

Signs that don't like to be tied down obviously have a head or heart start with Sagittarius, so Aquarius, Libra, and Gemini score well, while Aries and Leo spark brightly with this warm-blooded Fire sign. Fixed signs like Taurus and Capricorn find Sagittarius too fickle, while the Water signs are too moody. You have to be pretty thick-skinned to get along with Sagittarians because they don't know the meaning of tact. Many a would-be suitor has come out reeling from the frank answers given to questions like why they won't go out on a date.

It's a typical Sagittarian who burns the candle at both ends, so if you want to become involved with one, be prepared to dance the wee small hours away, play sport during the day, and for good measure, go camping on weekends. Sagittarians prefer the direct approach, enjoy frank discussions, and love animals. The race track or stables are the places to make contact with these "half horse" people. Hopeless with money, they will take you to the best place in town and starve the rest of the week. If you want to live life to the fullest, a Sagittarian is for you.

CAPRICORN

Capricorns are reserved and sometimes aloof, and it's difficult at times to know what they're thinking. Ms. Capricorn would no more ring up and ask a fellow out than fly in the air, so it's no good leaving her with a "See you around or give us a ring sometime" because she just doesn't work that way. She's a creature of propriety and has a very strict moral code that she adheres to. Although she may come over prim and proper, she has a great sense of humor and loves music and dancing. Don't expect her to do a solo number on the dance floor, though.

Mr. Goat has similar ethics and hates more than anything to be shown up. He will walk away if the partner he's with gets loud, noisy, or drinks too much. Parting a Capricorn from his money is a major operation, so if you love this sign, you may have to settle for beach barbecues, picnics, walks around the art gallery, or anything else that is minimal in cost.

Fellows stand to win if taking out a Capricorn lady because she knows a dollar doesn't go far, and she will also settle for somewhere that doesn't give the checkbook a nervous breakdown. This careful streak doesn't last forever—it's usually because Mr. or Ms. Goat is saving very hard for a nice home or furnishings, because they like to settle down and make nesting noises. So if you are a Taurus or Virgo or any of the Water signs, you'll be more than happy to skip the superficial enjoyments and assure yourself of a secure future.

Off-color jokes and language go down like a lead balloon with this sign as does exhibitionism, excessive drinking, and loose morals. Capricorns are found in abundance in banks, credit unions, and government health agencies.

AQUARIUS

Have you ever had the yearning to take a trip to the moon or go to outer space? Well, I've got news for you. You don't need to leave Mother Earth for this. As long as you have an Aquarius in tow, you'll live on another planet. First of all, you have to reprogram your thinking to get to first base with this spaced-out sign. Geminis and Libras have no trouble doing this as they're halfway there anyway, while the Fire signs are fascinated by them but strong enough to provide an anchor for them.

Taurus, Pisces, and Capricorn have little in common with Aquarians, so it's usually a case of unrequited love here. One of the early lessons one has to learn with this sign is how *not* to conform. The more eccentric you are, the better you'll get on with them. Clothes are another attraction, the weirder the better, so girls who've got their eye on a spunky Aquarian should wear gear that is exotic to be noticed. He won't want lasting relationships while he's out having a good time, so don't get heavy. Unfortunately, he doesn't know what jealousy means, so it's no good trying to get him jealous. He'll just bow out nicely and wish you the best.

Ms. Aquarius likes to be where it's all happening. Home is only for sleeping in; she's got to go out and taste life, so fellows need a lot of money and stamina to keep up with this whirling dervish. She's quite independent, so don't make the mistake of having a fight with her at the disco or she'll find her own way home.

This is a sign that loves futuristic things. Take Aquarians to see space movies or exhibitions that show houses or computers of the future. A little

reminder before you ask for a date: tell them you'll
be ready an hour earlier, this way you may get
out on time.

PISCES

Have you ever felt you were chasing your tail?
Well, imagine how a Pisces feels all the time. Poor
little fish, they swim in circles and go nowhere.
When someone spies a Pisces and sets out to
catch it, they have to bait the hook very carefully.
For instance, they are slippery little customers and
often don't want to be caught, so a modus ope-
randi is very necessary.

Pisces are suckers for sad stories, so appeal to
their sympathetic natures. Any girl will help a guy
who comes to her, heartbroken and lost, and a
Pisces male is a master at putting a convincing
story across. He hates to be organized, and the
bossy Fire signs—Leo, Aries, and Sagittarius—leave
him cold, and the hyperactive Air signs only ruffle
his tranquil little pond, usually causing him to
swim off to calmer waters, straight into the arms
of another waiting Water sign. The Earth signs,
Taurus, Capricorn, and Virgo, provide an anchor
for this drifting sign and therefore blend well.

Ms. Pisces has a deadly weapon: those eyes
with their long eyelashes melt the hardest heart
and, combined with the air of helpless femininity,
make a very soulful picture. Don't you believe it,
fellows. Behind that gentle little fish lies the mind

of a piranha, and you could be the one that is caught—hook, line, and sinker.

Most Pisceans hate noise, preferring dark secluded bars or clubs. A good place to meet this sign is at the local pool, beach, or just off the beaten track. It is not a greedy sign, and Pisceans are just as happy with a jug of wine, a loaf of bread, and you. Soft lights and sweet music are a necessary ingredient in this recipe for love, not to mention the sweet nothings.

THE AUTHOR

One of Australia's foremost astrologers and psychics, Bridget was born in England—a Taurus with a Gemini/Cancer ascendant. She follows a family tradition—her mother and grandmother were both psychics.

Married, with five children, Bridget manages to juggle her happy family life with a career that includes regular newspaper, radio, and television appearances, numerous private consultations (she has a reputation as an accurate predictor of stock market movements and horse races), frequent speaking at club functions, and an annual cruise as a guest lecturer and psychic.

Bridget's other books include *Bridget's Star Guide for Lovers*, *The ABC of ESP*, and *Bridget's Cusp Signs*.

YOUR GUIDE TO THE STARS

Bantam has a wide range of books on Astrology from which to choose. Check to see which titles are missing from your bookshelf.

☐ 27882 **LINDA GOODMAN'S SUN SIGNS** $5.95

☐ 34562 **LINDA GOODMAN'S SUN SIGNS (Large Format)** $12.95

☐ 27380 **ROBIN MACNAUGHTON'S SUN SIGN PERSONALITY GUIDE** $4.95

☐ 25849 **SECRETS FROM A STARGAZER'S NOTEBOOK, Debbi K. Smith** $4.95

☐ 27423 **SKYMATES, S & J Forrest** $4.50

☐ 34537 **ALAN OKEN'S ASTROLOGY** $13.95

EXPLORE THE SPIRITUAL WORLD WITH SHIRLEY MacLAINE AND JESS STEARN

Check to see which of these fine titles are missing from your bookshelf:

Titles by Jess Stearn:

☐ 26085 EDGAR CAYCE: SLEEPING PROPHET $4.50

☐ 25150 SOULMATES $3.95

☐ 26057 YOGA, YOUTH, AND REINCARNATION $3.95

Titles by Shirley MacLaine:

☐ 27557 DANCING IN THE LIGHT $4.95

☐ 27370 OUT ON A LIMB $4.95

☐ 27438 "DON'T FALL OFF THE MOUNTAIN" $4.95

☐ 26173 YOU CAN GET THERE FROM HERE $4.95

☐ 27299 IT'S ALL IN THE PLAYING $4.95

☐ 05367 GOING WITHIN $18.95

Look for them in your bookstore or use the coupon below:

Bantam Books, Dept. PW4, 414 East Golf Road, Des Plaines, IL 60016

Please send me the items I have checked above. I am enclosing $_____ (please add $2.00 to cover postage and handling). Send check or money order, no cash or C.O.D.s please.

Mr/Ms _____

Address _____

City/State _____ Zip _____

Please allow four to six weeks for delivery.
Prices and availability subject to change without notice.

PW4–11/89